Robert Schumann

(1810–1856)

Selected Works for Solo Piano
Volume II

Davidsbündlertänze (Second edition of 1850–51), Op. 6
Grand Sonata № 1 in F♯ minor, Op. 11
Grand Sonata № 2 in G minor, Op. 22
Grand Sonata № 3 in F minor (Second version of 1853), Op. 14
Fantasie, Op. 17
Novelletten, Op. 21
Carnival Jest from Vienna, Op. 26
Three Romances, Op. 28

URTEXT EDITION

Editor and Music Engraver:
Ephraim Hammett Jones

DOVER PUBLICATIONS, INC.
Mineola, New York

Bibliographical Note

This Dover edition, first published in 2012, is a newly engraved urtext compilation of works by
Robert Schumann, transcribed from early authoritative editions.

International Standard Book Number

ISBN-13: 978-0-486-49072-4
ISBN-10: 0-486-49072-6

Manufactured in the United States by Courier Corporation
49072601
www.doverpublications.com

Preface

ABOUT THIS EDITION

An edition of a musical composition that presents the intentions of the composer is what is known nowadays as an URTEXT or "original text." The concept that urtext editions represent what the composer originally wrote is not quite correct. For many 18th and 19th century works the composer's original manuscripts were lost or destroyed. Works lacking original manuscripts include many pieces by Mozart, Beethoven, Chopin, and other major composers. First editions, which were generally proofread by the composer, are the principal sources for the musical text in these cases. Sometimes, copies of first editions in the possession of a composer's student, colleague, friend, or patron may contain corrections and markings in the composer's handwriting. Early drafts and sketchbooks plus copies made for the music engraver, are sometimes used as supplemental sources. In some cases, composers marked their revisions on personal copies of printed scores, neglecting to insert them into the original manuscript.

By the 19th century, heavily revised editions of the works of major composers appeared in which phrasing, slurs, articulations and dynamics were added or changed according to how the editor thought the music was to be interpreted. The degree to which the original musical text was altered varied greatly from editor to editor. The complete editions of the music of Chopin edited by Karl Mikuli, and the works of Schumann edited by Clara Schumann, are both examples of exemplary 19th-century urtext editing at its best. In Schumann's case, Clara gave the premiere performance of many of his solo piano works and continued to perform them throughout her long career.

Since the mid-1900s, musicians have become more aware of editions in which the music has been "tampered" with and edited with a heavy hand. The primary source for the musical text for the present two volumes of selected piano works of Robert Schumann is the complete edition of his works edited by his widow Clara, published by Breitkopf & Härtel from 1881–1893. Based on manuscripts, first editions, the composer's personal copies and Clara's recollections, they are highly accurate and quite free of the arbitrary alterations which plague so many editions of that era. The main drawback to the Clara Schumann edition lies in its often crowded, dense music engraving, which tends to obscure important aspects of the notation. To ensure the best possible reading of some passages, every note of music has been thoroughly checked against modern urtext editions and their critical commentaries. The editor (who is also the engraver) has opted for a page layout that is spacious and easy on the eyes. Many passages where both left and right hand were written on the same staff have been divided between staves for easier reading. Every piece has been carefully fingered, a feature sorely missing in the original volumes (which included only the composer's very sparse fingering indications.) Dynamics, articulations and slurs which were sometimes missing or placed incorrectly, have been restored where necessary.

DAVIDSBÜNDLERTÄNZE (Second edition of 1850–51), Op. 6

The "Dances of the League of David" were composed in 1837 around the time Schumann became secretly engaged to Clara Wieck. This was a period of both happiness and turmoil for Schumann. Clara's father refused to give consent to the marriage, labeling Schumann a "penniless composer." Despite it's low opus number, the Davidsbündlertänze were composed after *Carnaval,* Op. 9, *Symphonic Etudes,* Op. 13, and *Fantasie,* Op. 17. Clara performed the work frequently, especially after Robert's death in 1856, and it was among the works she performed at her last public appearance in 1895. Schumann credited his alter egos Florestan and Eusebius with the creation of the two sets of nine dances in both the autograph and the first edition. In 1850–51 he published a second edition of the work in which he revised some of the music and removed all of the literary references in the first edition.

GRAND SONATA № 1, Op. 11, GRAND SONATA № 2, Op. 22, GRAND SONATA № 3, (Second version) Op. 14

Schumann's venture into the piano sonata form resulted in the creation of three published works with the title "Grand Sonata." The *Allegro,* Op. 8 was possibly the only surviving movement of an earlier attempt at the form, and the original concept of the *Fantasie,* Op. 17 was a sonata composed as a tribute to Beethoven. The legacy of Beethoven, in the realm of the piano sonata, weighed heavily on any composer venturing to write in this form after his death in 1827. Schumann spent much time on the *Grand Sonatas,* Op.11, Op. 22, and Op.14, rewriting movements, discarding movements, and in the case of the G minor sonata, replacing the last movement altogether.

The first sonata in F♯ minor contains motifs in the first movement that appear in one of Clara's published piano pieces. Two of the great pianists of that time—Ignaz Moscheles and Franz Liszt gave positive reviews of the first Sonata. Clara revived her interest in it late in her career, programming it on her recitals in the 1880s.

Much of the second sonata was written contemporaneously with the first, but because of numerous rewrites and, eventually, a reversion to what he originally wrote in the first movement, the publication of the second sonata was delayed until after the third, resulting in a higher opus number. The original final movement of the second sonata was long, complex and extremely difficult to play. Just before Schumann submitted it to be published, he received a letter from Clara expressing her concern about the last movement. Schumann agreed, discarded it, and wrote a movement that matched the tone of the first movement better. Clara adored the second sonata and performed it frequently throughout her career.

The third sonata was originally conceived as a five movement work but was published with only three of the five with the title *Concerto Without Orchestra*. In 1853 Schumann published a second version of this piece. Again it was conceived as a five movement work, but seems to have been pared down to four at the time it was submitted to the publisher. Much of the first movement was rewritten. The Scherzo II from the originally planned five movement work was substituted for the Scherzo I. The third movement lost two variations, and the final movement was extensively rewritten. This is the version presented in this edition.

FANTASIE, Op. 17

"Sonata for Beethoven" was the original title, in 1836, for the *Fantasie* Op. 17 and the proceeds of the initial sale of the work were destined to assist in the erection of a monument in honor of Beethoven by the Bonn Committee. The planned titles for the three movement work were "Ruins," "Trophies," and "Palms." Later, in 1838, while still revising the work he decided to title the work *Poem* and the movements "Ruins," "Victory Arch," and "Constellation." By the time Schumann submitted the work to Breitkopf & Härtel for publication in late 1838 he removed the movement names and titled the work simply *Fantasie*. In a letter to Clara in 1838 Schumann wrote, "The first movement is probably the most passionate I have ever written—a deep lamentation for you." Along with *Kreisleriana* Op. 16, the *Fantasie* represents the pinnacle of Schumann's artistic and creative genius in composing for piano solo.

NOVELLETTEN, Op. 21

The eight pieces that Schumann titled *Novelletten* were written over a short period of time during 1838, around the sane time he was composing the *Scenes from Childhood*. In a letter he called them "fairly lengthy interrelated adventure stories." Originally, some of the movements and even some sections of movements had descriptive titles which Schumann eventually removed when he was about to publish them, not wishing his music to be labeled "program music." In spite of calling them "interrelated" he encouraged Clara and even Franz Liszt to extract separate pieces from the set, which has become the standard practice for this work.

CARNIVAL JEST FROM VIENNA, Op. 26

Schumann traveled to Vienna in 1838 with the idea fixed in his mind to make it the future home for himself and his soon-to-be-wife, Clara. Less than a year later he was again in Leipzig having abandoned the idea of living in Vienna. Even though his expectations were not realized, his brief sojourn in Vienna was a fruitful one. The *Blumenstück*, *Humoreske* and *Novelletten* were all composed during this time, as well as preliminary work on the *Carnival Jest* which he completed later in Leipzig. The new work, published by Machetti in 1841, was described by Schumann in a letter to Clara as a "romantic spectacle" and was warmly received by the music critics.

THREE ROMANCES, Op. 28

Little is know about the composition of the *Three Romances*. They were probably composed during 1840, the year Robert was finally to wed his beloved Clara. They were married in spite of her father's objection on the day before her twenty-first birthday. Clara greatly admired the *Romances*, especially the second, which she called "the most beautiful love duet", and urged Robert to dedicate them to her as a wedding present. Schumannm however, dedicated the *Romances* to an admirer and friend. At first, Schumann had little regard for the *Romances*, but a few years later, he wrote to a friend that he considered them among his best pieces, along with the *Novelletten*, *Kreisleriana*, and *Phantasiestücke*.

Translation of German Tempo Markings and Expressions

Äußerst rasch und mit Bravour	Extremely rapidly and with bravura
Balladenmäßig	In the style of a ballad
Ballmäßig	In the style of a grand ball
Durchaus phantastisch und leidenschaftlich vorzutragen	Quite fantastically and passionately
Durchaus zart	Quite tenderly
Durchweg leise zu halten	Keep quiet throughout
Einfach	Simply
Einfach und gesangvoll	Simply and with a singing style
Erstes Tempo	First Tempo
Etwas bewegter	Somewhat more moving, *più mosso*
Etwas langsamer	Somewhat more slowly, *meno mosso*
Fortsetzung	Continuation
Fortsetzung und Schluss	Continuation and conclusion
Frisch	Brisk, lively
Getragen	Sustained, slow, *sostenuto*
Hell und lustig	Brightly and merrily
Höchst lebhaft	Most lively
Im lebhaften Tempo	In a lively tempo
Im Legendenton	In the tone of a legend
Immer lebendiger	Ever more lively
Immer schneller und schneller	Ever faster and faster
Innig	Intimately
Kurze Pause	Short break, pause
Langsam getragen	Slowly, solemn
Lebhaft	Lively
Leicht	Easily, lightly
Markiert und kräftig	Accented, *marcatto*, and forceful, *con forza*
Mässig, Durchaus energisch	Moderately, quite energetically
Mit größter Energie	With great energy
Mit gutem Humor	With good humor
Mit Humor	With humor
Munter, nicht zu rasch	Lively, not too rapidly

nach und nach bewegeter und schneller	gradually moving faster
nach und nach schneller	gradually faster
Nach und nach lebhafter	Gradually livelier
Nicht schnell	Not fast
Noch lebhafter	Still livelier
Noch schneller	Still faster
Rasch und wild	Rapidly and wildly
Rauschend und festlich	rustling, splashing and festive
Schneller	Faster
Sehr lebhaft	Very lively
Sehr lebhaft mit vielem Humor	Very lively with much humor
Sehr markiert	Very marked, accented, *marcatto*
Sehr munter	Very lively
Sehr rasch	Very rapidly
Sehr rasch und markiert	Very rapidly and accented, *marcatto*
So rasch wie möglich	As rapidly as possible
Stimme aus der Ferne	Voice from the distance
Tempo wie am Anfang	Tempo like at the beginning
Tempo wie im vorigen Stück	Speed as in the previous piece
Tempo wie vorher	Tempo like beforehand
Ungeduldig	Impatiently, *agitato*
Wie aus der Ferne	As from a distance
Wie früher	As previously
Wie vorher	Like beforehand
Wild und lustig	Wildly and merrily
Zart und singend	Tenderly and singing
Ziemlich langsam	Rather slowly

CONTENTS

N⁰ 6

Sehr lebhaft mit vielem Humor (♩ = 72)

II.

Einfach (♪ = 100)

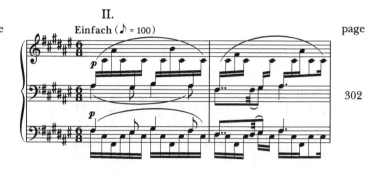

N⁰ 7

Äußerst rasch (♩. = 116)

III.

Sehr markiert (♩ = 138)

N⁰ 8

Sehr lebhaft (♩ = 100)

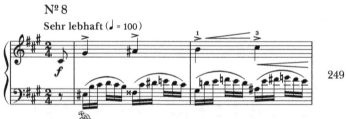

CARNIVAL JEST FROM VIENNA, OP. 26

FASCHINGSSCHWANK AUS WIEN

Sehr lebhaft ♩. = 76

THREE ROMANCES, OP. 28

I.

Sehr markiert (M.M. ♩ = 88)

Robert Schumann

(1810–1856)

Selected Works for Solo Piano
Volume II

URTEXT EDITION

Walther von Goethe zugeeignet

DAVIDSBÜNDLERTÄNZE

Eighteen Character Pieces

Second Edition, 1850–51

ROBERT SCHUMANN, Op. 6 (1837)

12

18

VIII.

Mit Humor (M.M. ♩ = 96)

XII.

Wild und lustig (M.M. ♩ = 152)

XIII.

ad lib. Da Capo
senza replica

XVI.

Mit gutem Humor (M.M. ♩ = 132)

Etwas langsamer

TRIO

Wie aus der Ferne (M.M. ♩ = 100)

XVII.

nach und nach schneller

Clara zugeeignet von Florestan und Eusebius

GRAND SONATA Nº 1

Robert Schumann, Op. 11 (1833–1835)

INTRODUZIONE
Un poco Adagio

ARIA

senza passione, ma espressivo

Pedale

semplice

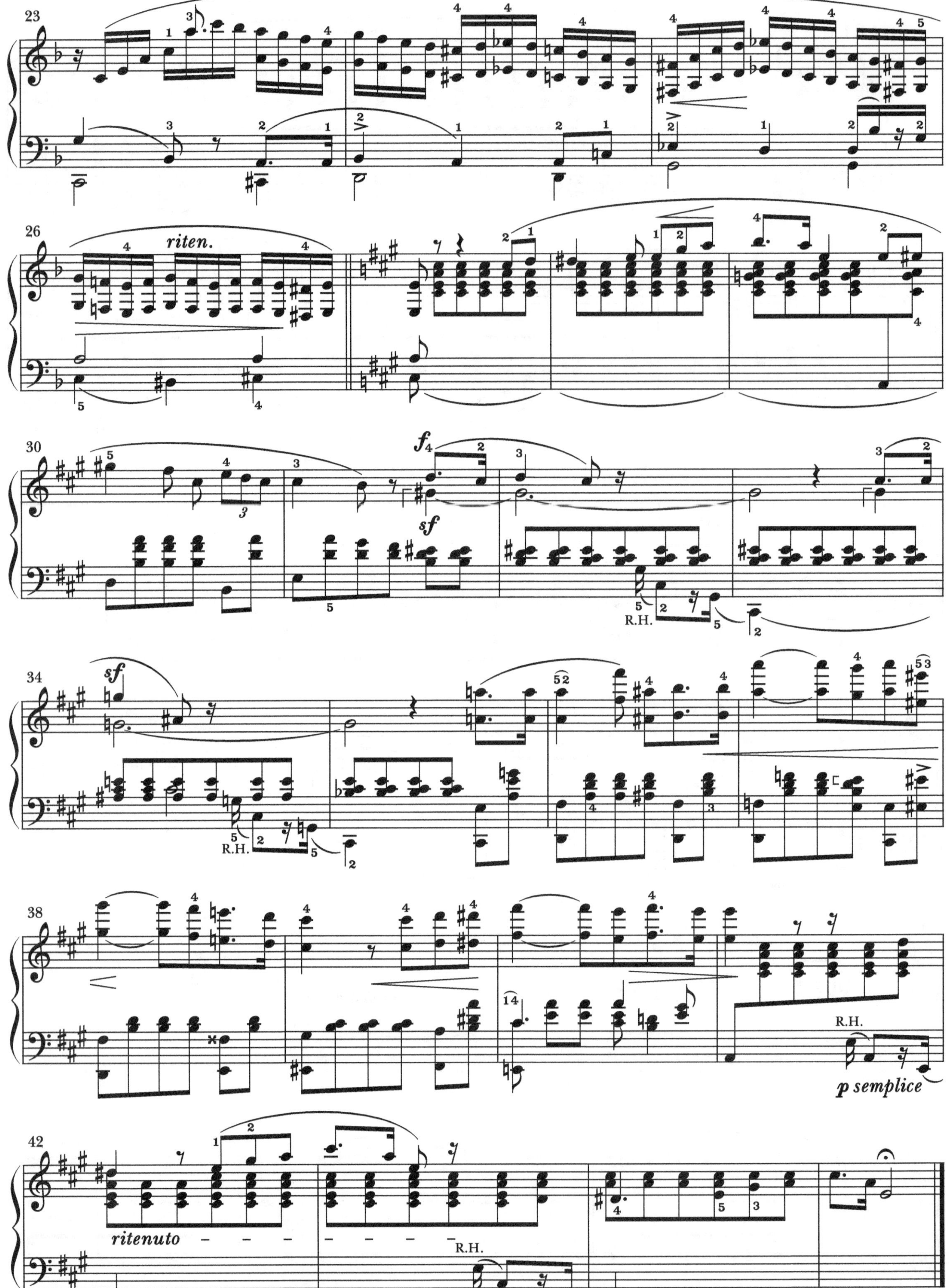
riten.
sf
R.H.
p semplice
ritenuto

SCHERZO E INTERMEZZO

INTERMEZZO

* m. 170: Fingering is by Schumann

FINALE

Allegro un poco maestoso

*In Schumann's personal copy of the first edition, he indicated a cut of measures 214–254 with a new transition for measure 213.

Madame Henriette Voigt geb. Kunze zugeeignet

GRAND SONATA №. 2

ROBERT SCHUMANN, Op. 22 (1830–37)

So rasch wie möglich M.M. ♩ = 144

* possibly E♭

SCHERZO

Sehr rasch und markiert M.M. ♩ = 138

RONDO

Presto M.M. ♩ = 160

Etwas langsamer

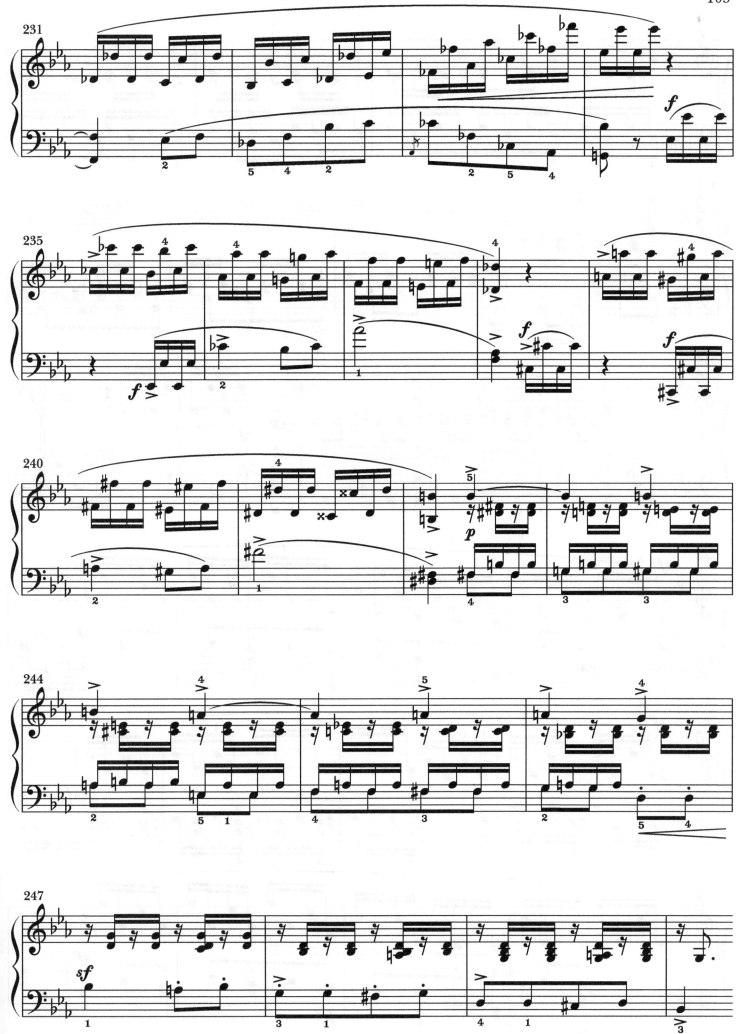

Prestissimo
Quasi Cadenza

à Monsieur Ignace Moscheles

GRAND SONATA № 3

Second Edition, 1853

ROBERT SCHUMANN, Op. 14 (1833–1835)

SCHERZO

Molto commodo ♩ = 116

QUASI VARIAZIONI

Andantino de Clara Wieck ♩ = 84

Molto a capriccio sem-

pre stringendo

Più presto

Vivacissimo

Franz Liszt gewidmet

FANTASIE

Durch alle Töne tönet
Im bunten Erdentraum
Ein leiser Ton gezogen
Für den der heimlich lauschet.
Fr. Schlegel

ROBERT SCHUMANN, Op. 17 (1835–36)

Durchaus phantastisch und leidenschaftlich vorzutragen M.M. ♩ = 80

Im lebhaften Tempo

Erstes Tempo

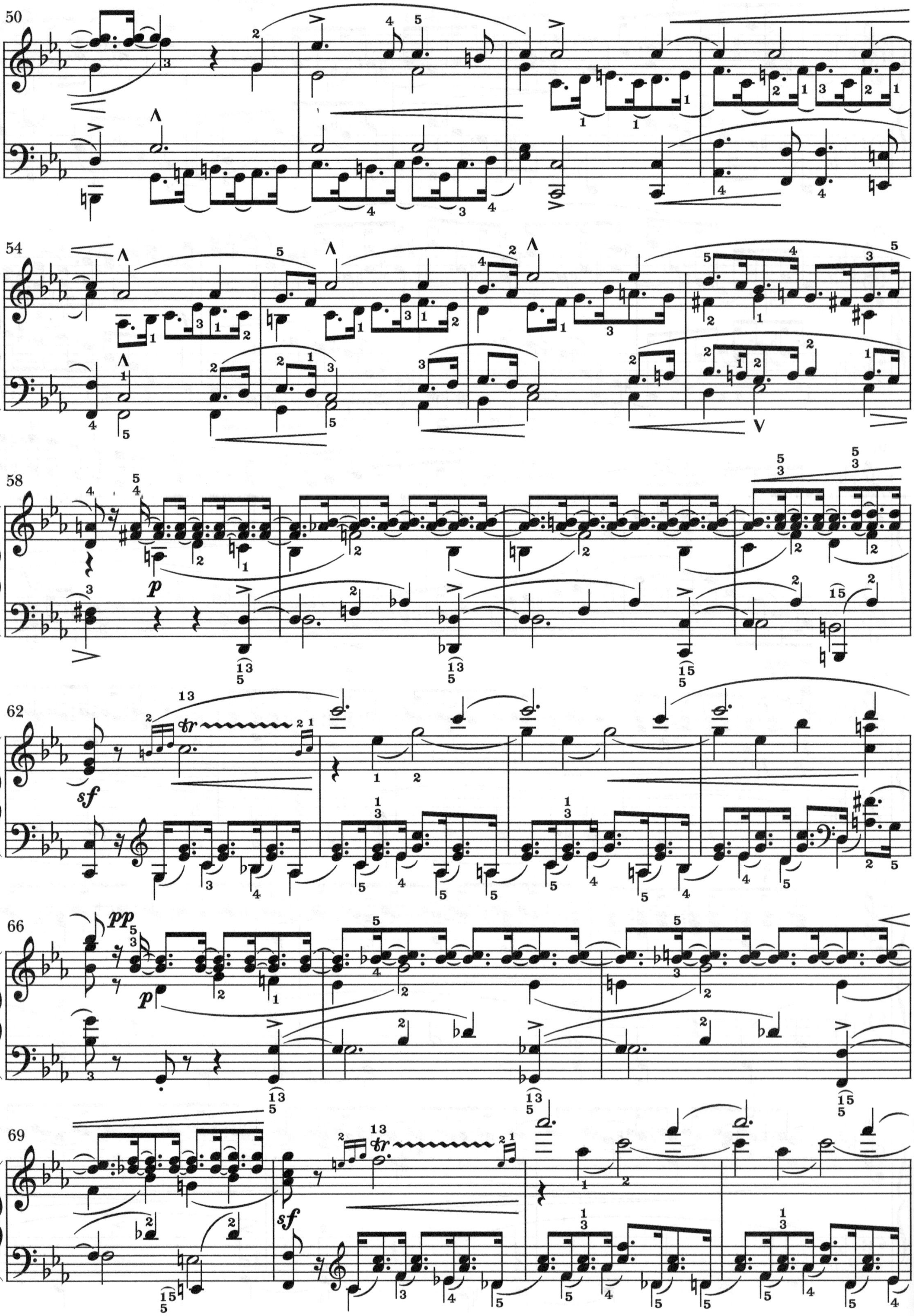
50
54
58
p
62
sf
66
pp
p
69
sf

Etwas langsamer

Pedal

Langsam getragen. Durchweg leise zu halten M.M. $\quad \bullet$. = 60

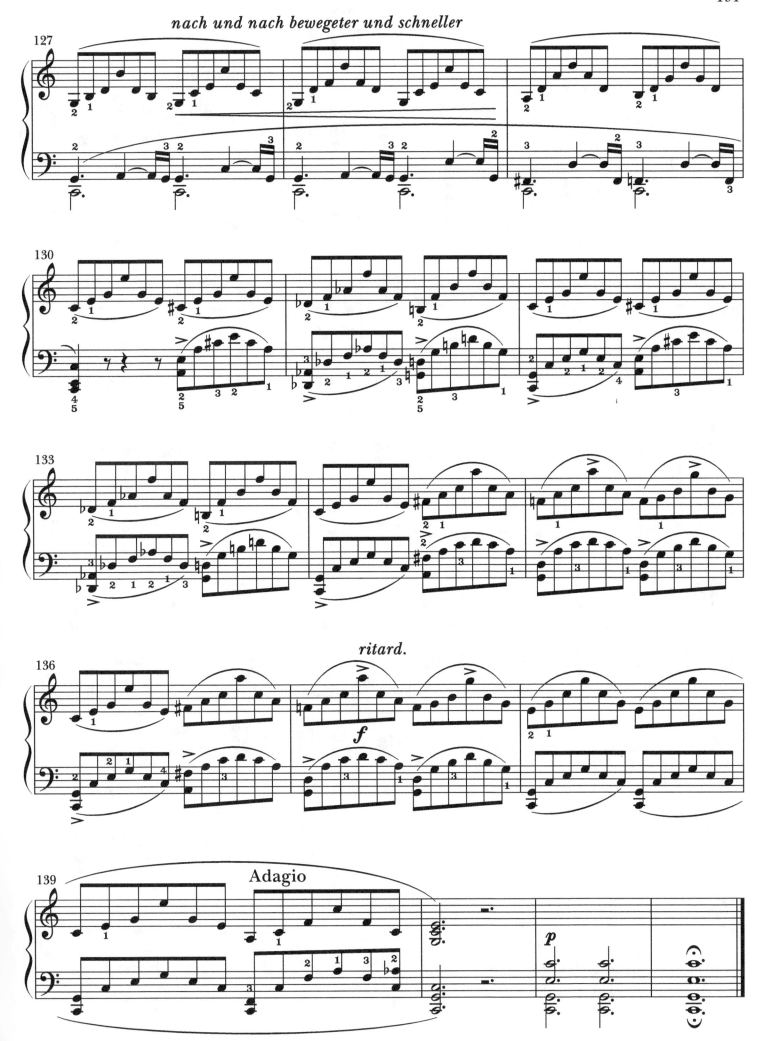

Adolph Henselt gewidmet

NOVELLETTEN

Robert Schumann, Op. 21 (1838)

HEFT I.

Markiert und kräftig (♩ = 108)

Nº 1.

INTERMEZZO
Etwas langsamer, durchaus zart (♩ = 104)

Leicht und mit Humor (♩ = 138)

Nº 3.

INTERMEZZO
Rasch und wild (♩. = 138)

Ballmäßig. Sehr munter (♩. = 66)

№ 4.

HEFT III.

Rauschend und festlich (♩ = 116)

Nº 5.

Etwas langsamer

Erstes Tempo

Immer schneller und schneller

TRIO I

TRIO II

Hell und lustig (♩ = 132)

256

Stimme aus der Ferne

FORTSETZUNG

FORTSETZUNG UND SCHLUSS

Munter, nicht zu rasch (♩ = 120) *

*An annotation in the original edition reads: "The tempo faster and faster to the end."

Simonin de Sire in Dinant zugeeignet

CARNIVAL JEST FROM VIENNA

FASCHINGSSCHWANK AUS WIEN

Fantastic Pictures | Phantasiebilder

Robert Schumann, Op. 26 (1839)

I. Allegro

II. Romanze

Ziemlich langsam M.M. ♪ = 92

III. Scherzino

IV. Intermezzo

Mit größter Energie M.M. ♩ = 116

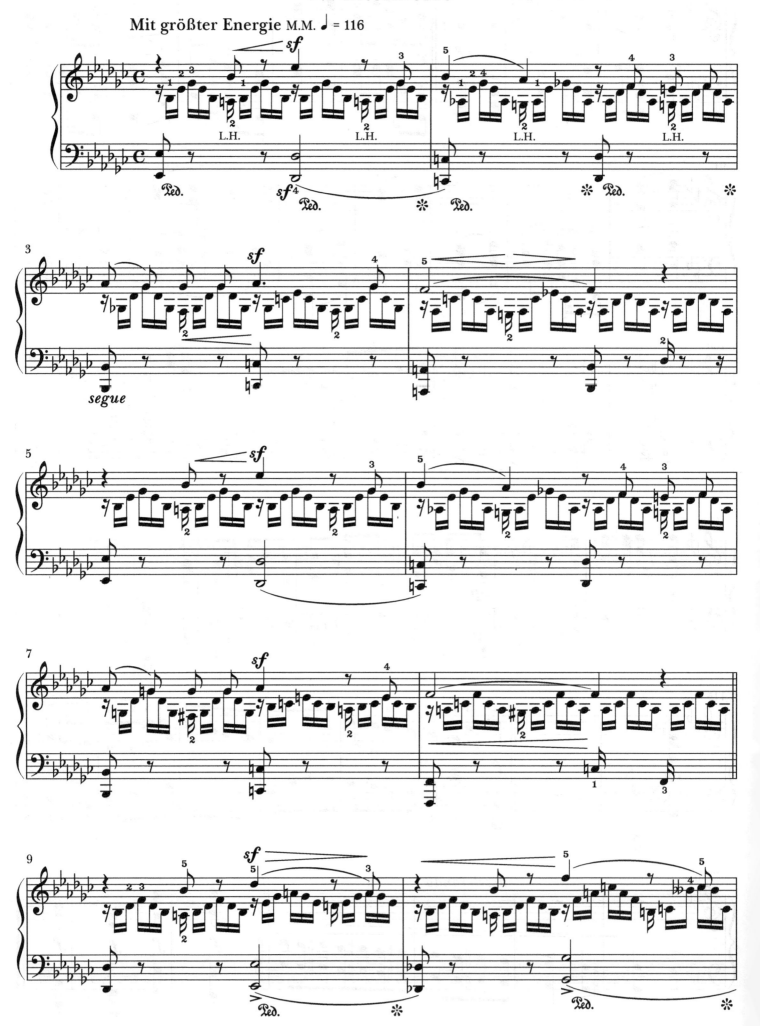

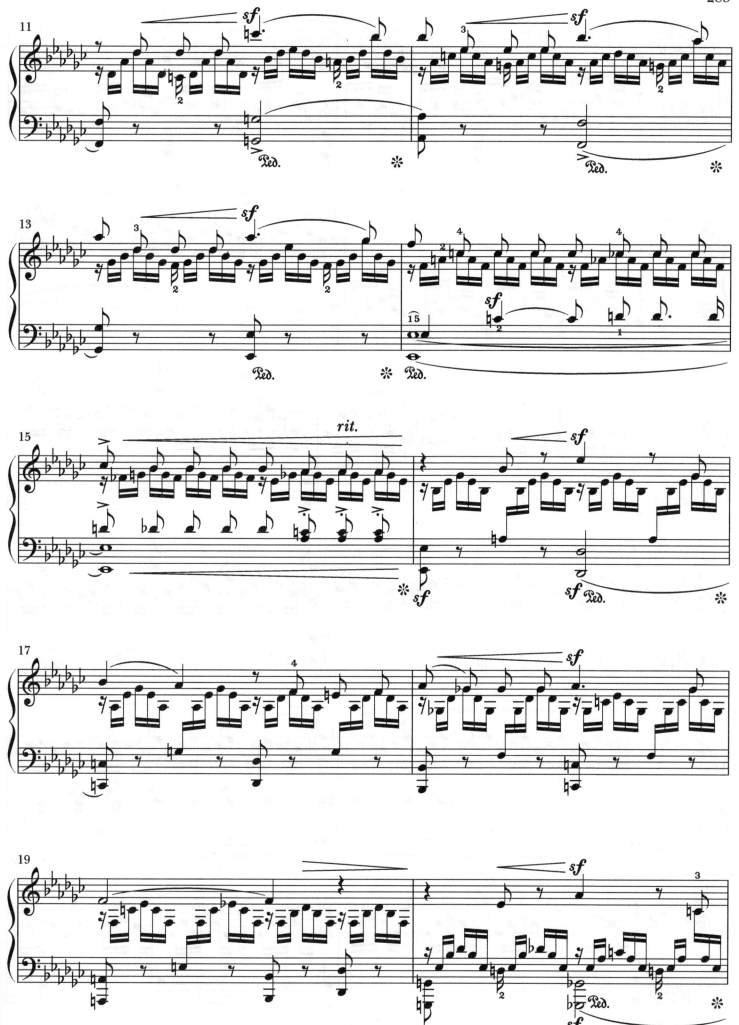

V. Finale

Graf Heinrich II. Reuß - Köstritz gewidmet

THREE ROMANCES
DREI ROMANZEN

ROBERT SCHUMANN, Op. 28 (1839)

I.

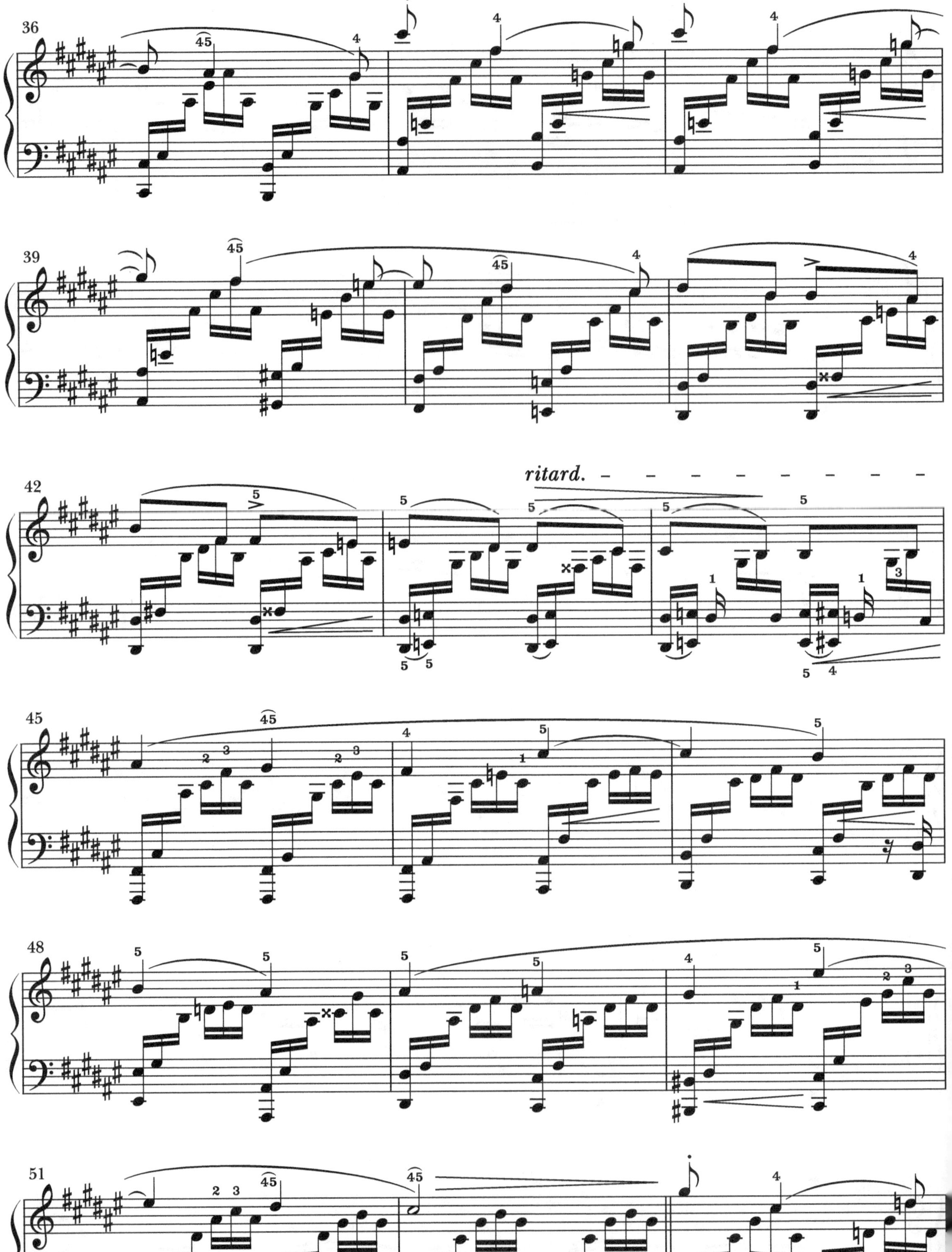
ritard.

II.

III.

INTERMEZZO I

INTERMEZZO II

Etwas langsamer

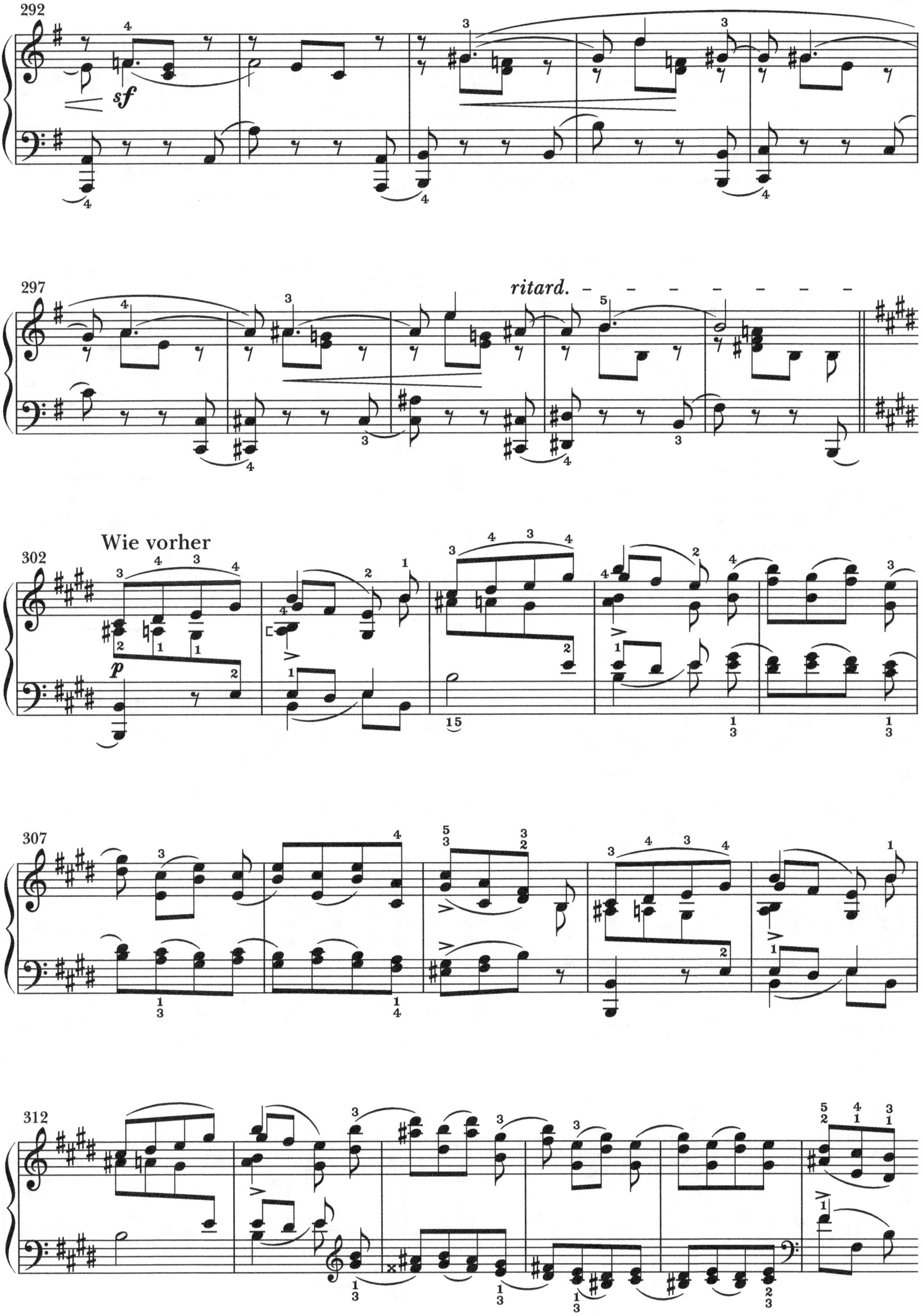

292
sf
297
ritard.
302
Wie vorher
p
307
312

Dover Piano and Keyboard Editions

Albeniz, Isaac, IBERIA AND ESPAÑA: Two Complete Works for Solo Piano. Spanish composer's greatest piano works in authoritative editions. Includes the popular "Tango." 192pp. 9 x 12.   0-486-25367-8

Bach, Johann Sebastian, COMPLETE KEYBOARD TRANSCRIPTIONS OF CONCERTOS BY BAROQUE COMPOSERS. Sixteen concertos by Vivaldi, Telemann and others, transcribed for solo keyboard instruments. Bach-Gesellschaft edition. 128pp. 9⅜ x 12¼.   0-486-25529-8

Bach, Johann Sebastian, COMPLETE PRELUDES AND FUGUES FOR ORGAN. All 25 of Bach's complete sets of preludes and fugues (i.e. compositions written as pairs), from the authoritative Bach-Gesellschaft edition. 168pp. 8⅜ x 11.   0-486-24816-X

Bach, Johann Sebastian, ITALIAN CONCERTO, CHROMATIC FANTASIA AND FUGUE AND OTHER WORKS FOR KEYBOARD. Sixteen of Bach's best-known, most-performed and most-recorded works for the keyboard, reproduced from the authoritative Bach-Gesellschaft edition. 112pp. 9 x 12.   0-486-25387-2

Bach, Johann Sebastian, KEYBOARD MUSIC. Bach-Gesellschaft edition. For harpsichord, piano, other keyboard instruments. English Suites, French Suites, Six Partitas, Goldberg Variations, Two-Part Inventions, Three-Part Sinfonias. 312pp. 8⅛ x 11.   0-486-22360-4

Bach, Johann Sebastian, ORGAN MUSIC. Bach-Gesellschaft edition. 93 works. 6 Trio Sonatas, German Organ Mass, Orgelbüchlein, Six Schubler Chorales, 18 Choral Preludes. 357pp. 8⅛ x 11.   0-486-22359-0

Bach, Johann Sebastian, TOCCATAS, FANTASIAS, PASSACAGLIA AND OTHER WORKS FOR ORGAN. Over 20 best-loved works including Toccata and Fugue in D Minor, BWV 565; Passacaglia and Fugue in C Minor, BWV 582, many more. Bach-Gesellschaft edition. 176pp. 9 x 12.   0-486-25403-8

Bach, Johann Sebastian, TWO- AND THREE-PART INVENTIONS. Reproduction of original autograph ms. Edited by Eric Simon. 62pp. 8⅛ x 11.   0-486-21982-8

Bach, Johann Sebastian, THE WELL-TEMPERED CLAVIER: Books I and II, Complete. All 48 preludes and fugues in all major and minor keys. Authoritative Bach-Gesellschaft edition. Explanation of ornaments in English, tempo indications, music corrections. 208pp. 9⅜ x 12¼.   0-486-24532-2

Bartók, Béla, PIANO MUSIC OF BÉLA BARTÓK, Series I. New, definitive Archive Edition incorporating composer's corrections. Includes *Funeral March* from *Kossuth, Fourteen Bagatelles,* Bartók's break to modernism. 167pp. 9 x 12. (Available in U.S. only)   0-486-24108-4

Bartók, Béla, PIANO MUSIC OF BÉLA BARTÓK, Series II. Second in the Archive Edition incorporating composer's corrections. 85 short pieces *For Children, Two Elegies, Two Romanian Dances,* etc. 192pp. 9 x 12. (Available in U.S. only)   0-486-24109-2

Beethoven, Ludwig van, BAGATELLES, RONDOS AND OTHER SHORTER WORKS FOR PIANO. Most popular and most performed shorter works, including Rondo a capriccio in G and Andante in F. Breitkopf & Härtel edition. 128pp. 9⅜ x 12¼.   0-486-25392-9

Beethoven, Ludwig van, COMPLETE PIANO SONATAS. All sonatas in fine Schenker edition, with fingering, analytical material. One of best modern editions. 615pp. 9 x 12. Two-vol. set.   0-486-23134-8, 0-486-23135-6

Beethoven, Ludwig van, COMPLETE VARIATIONS FOR SOLO PIANO, Ludwig van Beethoven. Contains all 21 sets of Beethoven's piano variations, including the extremely popular *Diabelli Variations, Op. 120.* 240pp. 9⅜ x 12¼.   0-486-25188-8

Beethoven, Ludwig van, BEETHOVEN MASTERPIECES FOR SOLO PIANO: 25 Works. Twenty-five popular pieces include the Sonata in C-sharp Minor, Op. 27, No. 2 ("Moonlight"); Sonata in D Minor, Op. 31, No. 2 ("Tempest"); 32 Variations in C Minor; Andante in F Major; Rondo Capriccio, Op. 129; Fantasia, Op. 77; and popular bagatelles, rondos, minuets, and other works. 160pp. 9 x 12.   0-486-43570-9

Blesh, Rudi (ed.), CLASSIC PIANO RAGS. Best ragtime music (1897–1922) by Scott Joplin, James Scott, Joseph F. Lamb, Tom Turpin, nine others. 364pp. 9 x 12. Introduction by Blesh.   0-486-20469-3

Brahms, Johannes, COMPLETE SHORTER WORKS FOR SOLO PIANO. All solo music not in other two volumes. Waltzes, Scherzo in E Flat Minor, Eight Pieces, Rhapsodies, Fantasies, Intermezzi, etc. Vienna Gesellschaft der Musikfreunde. 180pp. 9 x 12.   0-486-22651-4

Brahms, Johannes, COMPLETE SONATAS AND VARIATIONS FOR SOLO PIANO. All sonatas, five variations on themes from Schumann, Paganini, Handel, etc. Vienna Gesellschaft der Musikfreunde edition. 178pp. 9 x 12.   0-486-22650-6

Brahms, Johannes, COMPLETE TRANSCRIPTIONS, CADENZAS AND EXERCISES FOR SOLO PIANO. Vienna Gesellschaft der Musikfreunde edition, vol. 15. Studies after Chopin, Weber, Bach; gigues, sarabandes; 10 Hungarian dances, etc. 178pp. 9 x 12.   0-486-22652-2

Byrd, William, MY LADY NEVELLS BOOKE OF VIRGINAL MUSIC. 42 compositions in modern notation from 1591 ms. For any keyboard instrument. 245pp. 8⅛ x 11.   0-486-22246-2

Chopin, Frédéric, COMPLETE BALLADES, IMPROMPTUS AND SONATAS. The four Ballades, four Impromptus and three Sonatas. Authoritative Mikuli edition. 192pp. 9 x 12.   0-486-24164-5

Chopin, Frédéric, COMPLETE MAZURKAS, Frédéric Chopin. 51 best-loved compositions, reproduced directly from the authoritative Kistner edition edited by Carl Mikuli. 160pp. 9 x 12.   0-486-25548-4

Chopin, Frédéric, COMPLETE PRELUDES AND ETUDES FOR SOLO PIANO. All 25 Preludes and all 27 Etudes by greatest piano music composer. Authoritative Mikuli edition. 192pp. 9 x 12.   0-486-24052-5

Chopin, Frédéric, FANTASY IN F MINOR, BARCAROLLE, BERCEUSE AND OTHER WORKS FOR SOLO PIANO. 15 works, including one of the greatest of the Romantic period, the Fantasy in F Minor, Op. 49, reprinted from the authoritative German edition prepared by Chopin's student, Carl Mikuli. 224pp. 8⅜ x 11¼.   0-486-25950-1

Chopin, Frédéric, CHOPIN MASTERPIECES FOR SOLO PIANO: 46 Works. Includes Ballade No. 1 in G Minor, Berceuse, 3 ecossaises, 5 etudes, Fantaisie-Impromptu, Marche Funèbre, 8 mazurkas, 7 nocturnes, 3 polonaises, 9 preludes, Scherzo No. 2 in B-flat Minor, and 6 waltzes. Authoritative sources. 224pp. 9 x 12.   0-486-40150-2

Chopin, Frédéric, NOCTURNES AND POLONAISES. 20 *Nocturnes* and 11 *Polonaises* reproduced from the authoritative Mikuli edition for pianists, students, and musicologists. Commentary. 224pp. 9 x 12.   0-486-24564-0

Chopin, Frédéric, WALTZES AND SCHERZOS. All of the Scherzos and nearly all (20) of the Waltzes from the authoritative Mikuli edition. Editorial commentary. 160pp. 9 x 12.   0-486-24316-8

Cofone, Charles J. F. (ed.), ELIZABETH ROGERS HIR VIRGINALL BOOKE. All 112 pieces from noted 1656 manuscript, most never before published. Composers include Thomas Brewer, William Byrd, Orlando Gibbons, etc. Calligraphy by editor. 125pp. 9 x 12.   0-486-23138-0

*Available from your music dealer or write for **free** Music Catalog to*
Dover Publications, Inc., Dept. MUBI, 31 East 2nd Street, Mineola, NY 11501
*Visit us online at **www.doverpublications.com***

Dover Piano and Keyboard Editions

Couperin, François, KEYBOARD WORKS/Series One: Ordres I–XIII; Series Two: Ordres XIV–XXVII and Miscellaneous Pieces. Over 200 pieces. Reproduced directly from edition prepared by Johannes Brahms and Friedrich Chrysander. Total of 496pp. 8⅛ x 11.
Series I: 0-486-25795-9; Series II: 0-486-25796-7

Debussy, Claude, COMPLETE PRELUDES, Books 1 and 2. 24 evocative works that reveal the essence of Debussy's genius for musical imagery, among them many of the composer's most famous piano compositions. Glossary of French terms. 128pp. 8⅜ x 11¼.
0-486-25970-6

Debussy, Claude, DEBUSSY MASTERPIECES FOR SOLO PIANO: 20 Works. From France's most innovative and influential composer—a rich compilation of works that include "Golliwogg's cakewalk," "Engulfed cathedral," "Clair de lune," and 17 others. 128pp. 9 x 12. 0-486-42425-1

Debussy, Claude, PIANO MUSIC 1888–1905. Deux Arabesques, Suite Bergamasque, Masques, first series of Images, etc. Nine others, in corrected editions. 175pp. 9⅜ x 12¼.
0-486-22771-5

Dvořák, Antonín, HUMORESQUES AND OTHER WORKS FOR SOLO PIANO. Humoresques, Op. 101, complete, Silhouettes, Op. 8, Poetic Tone Pictures, Theme with Variations, Op. 36, 4 Slavonic Dances, more. 160pp. 9 x 12.
0-486-28355-0

de Falla, Manuel, AMOR BRUJO AND EL SOMBRERO DE TRES PICOS FOR SOLO PIANO. With these two popular ballets, El Amor Brujo (Love, the Magician) and El Sombrero de Tres Picos (The Three-Cornered Hat), Falla brought the world's attention to the music of Spain. The composer himself made these arrangements of the complete ballets for piano solo. xii+132pp. 9 x 12.
0-486-44170-9

Fauré, Gabriel, COMPLETE PRELUDES, IMPROMPTUS AND VALSES-CAPRICES. Eighteen elegantly wrought piano works in authoritative editions. Only one-volume collection available. 144pp. 9 x 12. (Not available in France or Germany)
0-486-25789-4

Fauré, Gabriel, NOCTURNES AND BARCAROLLES FOR SOLO PIANO. 12 nocturnes and 12 barcarolles reprinted from authoritative French editions. 208pp. 9⅜ x 12¼. (Not available in France or Germany)
0-486-27955-3

Feofanov, Dmitry (ed.), RARE MASTERPIECES OF RUSSIAN PIANO MUSIC: Eleven Pieces by Glinka, Balakirev, Glazunov and Others. Glinka's Prayer, Balakirev's Reverie, Liapunov's Transcendental Etude, Op. 11, No. 10, and eight others—full, authoritative scores from Russian texts. 144pp. 9 x 12.
0-486-24659-0

Franck, César, ORGAN WORKS. Composer's best-known works for organ, including Six Pieces, Trois Pieces, and Trois Chorals. Oblong format for easy use at keyboard. Authoritative Durand edition. 208pp. 11⅜ x 8¼.
0-486-25517-4

Gottschalk, Louis M., PIANO MUSIC. 26 pieces (including covers) by early 19th-century American genius. "Bamboula," "The Banjo," other Creole, Negro-based material, through elegant salon music. 301pp. 9¼ x 12.
0-486-21683-7

Granados, Enrique, GOYESCAS, SPANISH DANCES AND OTHER WORKS FOR SOLO PIANO. Great Spanish composer's most admired, most performed suites for the piano, in definitive Spanish editions. 176pp. 9 x 12.
0-486-25481-X

Grieg, Edvard, COMPLETE LYRIC PIECES FOR PIANO. All 66 pieces from Grieg's ten sets of little mood pictures for piano, favorites of generations of pianists. 224pp. 9⅜ x 12¼.
0-486-26176-X

Handel, G. F., KEYBOARD WORKS FOR SOLO INSTRUMENTS. 35 neglected works from Handel's vast oeuvre, originally jotted down as improvisations. Includes Eight Great Suites, others. New sequence. 174pp. 9⅜ x 12¼.
0-486-24338-9

Haydn, Joseph, COMPLETE PIANO SONATAS. 52 sonatas reprinted from authoritative Breitkopf & Härtel edition. Extremely clear and readable; ample space for notes, analysis. 464pp. 9⅜ x 12¼.
Vol. I: 0-486-24726-0; Vol. II: 0-486-24727-9

Jasen, David A. (ed.), RAGTIME GEMS: Original Sheet Music for 25 Ragtime Classics. Includes original sheet music and covers for 25 rags, including three of Scott Joplin's finest: "Searchlight Rag," "Rose Leaf Rag," and "Fig Leaf Rag." 122pp. 9 x 12.
0-486-25248-5

Joplin, Scott, COMPLETE PIANO RAGS. All 38 piano rags by the acknowledged master of the form, reprinted from the publisher's original editions complete with sheet music covers. Introduction by David A. Jasen. 208pp. 9 x 12.
0-486-25807-6

Liszt, Franz, ANNÉES DE PÈLERINAGE, COMPLETE. Authoritative Russian edition of piano masterpieces: Première Année (Suisse): Deuxième Année (Italie) and Venezia e Napoli; Troisième Année, other related pieces. 288pp. 9⅜ x 12¼.
0-486-25627-8

Liszt, Franz, BEETHOVEN SYMPHONIES NOS. 6–9 TRANSCRIBED FOR SOLO PIANO. Includes Symphony No. 6 in F major, Op. 68, "Pastorale"; Symphony No. 7 in A major, Op. 92; Symphony No. 8 in F major, Op. 93; and Symphony No. 9 in D minor, Op. 125, "Choral." A memorable tribute from one musical genius to another. 224pp. 9 x 12. 0-486-41884-7

Liszt, Franz, COMPLETE ETUDES FOR SOLO PIANO, Series I: Including the Transcendental Etudes, edited by Busoni. Also includes Etude in 12 Exercises, 12 Grandes Etudes and Mazeppa. Breitkopf & Härtel edition. 272pp. 8⅜ x 11¼.
0-486-25815-7

Liszt, Franz, COMPLETE ETUDES FOR SOLO PIANO, Series II: Including the Paganini Etudes and Concert Etudes, edited by Busoni. Also includes Morceau de Salon, Ab Irato. Breitkopf & Härtel edition. 192pp. 8⅜ x 11¼.
0-486-25816-5

Liszt, Franz, COMPLETE HUNGARIAN RHAPSODIES FOR SOLO PIANO. All 19 Rhapsodies reproduced directly from authoritative Russian edition. All headings, footnotes translated to English. 224pp. 8⅜ x 11¼.
0-486-24744-9

Liszt, Franz, LISZT MASTERPIECES FOR SOLO PIANO: 13 Works. Masterworks by the supreme piano virtuoso of the 19th century: Hungarian Rhapsody No. 2 in C-sharp minor, Consolation No. 3 in D-Flat major, Liebestraum No. 3 in A-flat major, La Campanella (Paganini Etude No. 3), and nine others. 128pp. 9 x 12.
0-486-41379-9

Liszt, Franz, MEPHISTO WALTZ AND OTHER WORKS FOR SOLO PIANO. Rapsodie Espagnole, Liebesträume Nos. 1–3, Valse Oubliée No. 1, Nuages Gris, Polonaises Nos. 1 and 2, Grand Galop Chromatique, more. 192pp. 8⅜ x 11¼.
0-486-28147-7

Liszt, Franz, PIANO TRANSCRIPTIONS FROM FRENCH AND ITALIAN OPERAS. Virtuoso transformations of themes by Mozart, Verdi, Bellini, other masters, into unforgettable music for piano. Published in association with American Liszt Society. 247pp. 9 x 12. 0-486-24273-0

Maitland, J. Fuller, Squire, W. B. (eds.), THE FITZWILLIAM VIRGINAL BOOK. Famous early 17th-century collection of keyboard music, 300 works by Morley, Byrd, Bull, Gibbons, etc. Modern notation. Total of 938pp. 8⅜ x 11. Two-vol. set. 0-486-21068-5, 0-486-21069-3

Medtner, Nikolai, COMPLETE FAIRY TALES FOR SOLO PIANO. Thirty-eight complex, surprising pieces by an underrated Russian 20th-century Romantic whose music is more cerebral and harmonically adventurous than Rachmaninoff's. 272pp. 9 x 12. (Available in U.S. only)
0-486-41683-6

Dover Piano and Keyboard Editions

Mendelssohn, Felix, COMPLETE WORKS FOR PIANOFORTE SOLO. Breitkopf and Härtel edition of Capriccio in F# Minor, Sonata in E Major, Fantasy in F# Minor, Three Caprices, Songs without Words, and 20 other works. Total of 416pp. 9⅜ x 12¼. Two-vol. set.
0-486-23136-4, 0-486-23137-2

Mozart, Wolfgang Amadeus, MOZART MASTERPIECES: 19 WORKS FOR SOLO PIANO. Superb assortment includes sonatas, fantasies, variations, rondos, minuets, and more. Highlights include "Turkish Rondo," "Sonata in C," and a dozen variations on "Ah, vous dirai-je, Maman" (the familiar tune "Twinkle, Twinkle, Little Star"). Convenient, attractive, inexpensive volume; authoritative sources. 128pp. 9 x 12.   0-486-40408-0

Pachelbel, Johann, THE FUGUES ON THE MAGNIFICAT FOR ORGAN OR KEYBOARD. 94 pieces representative of Pachelbel's magnificent contribution to keyboard composition; can be played on the organ, harpsichord or piano. 100pp. 9 x 12. (Available in U.S. only)
0-486-25037-7

Phillipp, Isidor (ed.), FRENCH PIANO MUSIC, AN ANTHOLOGY. 44 complete works, 1670–1905, by Lully, Couperin, Rameau, Alkan, Saint-Saëns, Delibes, Bizet, Godard, many others; favorite and lesser-known examples, all top quality. 188pp. 9 x 12. (Not available in France or Germany)   0-486-23381-2

Prokofiev, Sergei, PIANO SONATAS NOS. 1–4, OPP. 1, 14, 28, 29. Includes the dramatic Sonata No. 1 in F minor; Sonata No. 2 in D minor, a masterpiece in four movements; Sonata No. 3 in A minor, a brilliant 7-minute score; and Sonata No. 4 in C minor, a three-movement sonata considered vintage Prokofiev. 96pp. 9 x 12. (Available in U.S. only)   0-486-42128-7

Rachmaninoff, Serge, COMPLETE PRELUDES AND ETUDES-TABLEAUX. Forty-one of his greatest works for solo piano, including the riveting C Minor, G Minor and B Minor preludes, in authoritative editions. 208pp. 8⅜ x 11¼.   0-486-25696-0

Ravel, Maurice, PIANO MASTERPIECES OF MAURICE RAVEL. Handsome affordable treasury; *Pavane pour une infante defunte, jeux d'eau, Sonatine, Miroirs,* more. 128pp. 9 x 12. (Not available in France or Germany)
0-486-25137-3

Satie, Erik, GYMNOPÉDIES, GNOSSIENNES AND OTHER WORKS FOR PIANO. The largest Satie collection of piano works yet published, 17 in all, reprinted from the original French editions. 176pp. 9 x 12. (Not available in France or Germany)   0-486-25978-1

Satie, Erik, TWENTY SHORT PIECES FOR PIANO (Sports et Divertissements). French master's brilliant thumbnail sketches—verbal and musical—of various outdoor sports and amusements. English translations, 20 illustrations. Rare, limited 1925 edition. 48pp. 12 x 8⅞. (Not available in France or Germany)   0-486-24365-6

Scarlatti, Domenico, GREAT KEYBOARD SONATAS, Series I and Series II. 78 of the most popular sonatas reproduced from the G. Ricordi edition edited by Alessandro Longo. Total of 320pp. 8⅜ x 11¼.
Series I: 0-486-24996-4; Series II: 0-486-25003-2

Schubert, Franz, COMPLETE SONATAS FOR PIANOFORTE SOLO. All 15 sonatas. Breitkopf and Härtel edition. 293pp. 9⅜ x 12¼.
0-486-22647-6

Schubert, Franz, DANCES FOR SOLO PIANO. Over 350 waltzes, minuets, landler, ecossaises, and other charming, melodic dance compositions reprinted from the authoritative Breitkopf & Härtel edition. 192pp. 9⅜ x 12¼.
0-486-26107-7

Schubert, Franz, FIVE FAVORITE PIANO SONATAS. Here in one convenient, affordable volume are five great sonatas, including his last three, among the finest works ever composed for piano: *Sonata in C Minor, D. 958, A Major, D. 959,* and *B-flat Major, D. 960.* Also included are the sonatas in *A Minor, D. 784,* and *A Major, D. 664.* vi+122pp. 9 x 12.   0-486-44141-5

Schubert, Franz, SELECTED PIANO WORKS FOR FOUR HANDS. 24 separate pieces (16 most popular titles): Three Military Marches, Lebens-stürme, Four Polonaises, Four Ländler, etc. Rehearsal numbers added. 273pp. 9 x 12.   0-486-23529-7

Schubert, Franz, SHORTER WORKS FOR PIANOFORTE SOLO. All piano music except Sonatas, Dances, and a few unfinished pieces. Contains Wanderer, Impromptus, Moments Musicals, Variations, Scherzi, etc. Breitkopf and Härtel edition. 199pp. 9⅜ x 12¼.   0-486-22648-4

Schumann, Clara (ed.), PIANO MUSIC OF ROBERT SCHUMANN, Series I. Major compositions from the period 1830–39; *Papillons,* Toccata, Grosse Sonate No. 1, *Phantasiestücke, Arabeske, Blumenstück,* and nine other works. Reprinted from Breitkopf & Härtel edition. 274pp. 9⅜ x 12¼.
0-486-21459-1

Schumann, Clara (ed.), PIANO MUSIC OF ROBERT SCHUMANN, Series II. Major compositions from period 1838–53; *Humoreske, Novelletten,* Sonate No. 2, 43 *Clavierstücke für die Jugend,* and six other works. Reprinted from Breitkopf & Härtel edition. 272pp. 9⅜ x 12¼.   0-486-21461-3

Schumann, Clara (ed.), PIANO MUSIC OF ROBERT SCHUMANN, Series III. All solo music not in other two volumes, including *Symphonic Etudes, Phantaisie,* 13 other choice works. Definitive Breitkopf & Härtel edition. 224pp. 9⅜ x 12¼.   0-486-23906-3

Scriabin, Alexander, COMPLETE PIANO SONATAS. All ten of Scriabin's sonatas, reprinted from an authoritative early Russian edition. 256pp. 8⅜ x 11¼.   0-486-25850-5

Scriabin, Alexander, THE COMPLETE PRELUDES AND ETUDES FOR PIANOFORTE SOLO. All the preludes and etudes including many perfectly spun miniatures. Edited by K. N. Igumnov and Y. I. Mil'shteyn. 250pp. 9 x 12.   0-486-22919-X

Sousa, John Philip, SOUSA'S GREAT MARCHES IN PIANO TRANSCRIPTION. Playing edition includes: "The Stars and Stripes Forever," "King Cotton," "Washington Post," much more. 24 illustrations. 111pp. 9 x 12.   0-486-23132-1

Strauss, Johann, Jr., FAVORITE WALTZES, POLKAS AND OTHER DANCES FOR SOLO PIANO. "Blue Danube," "Tales from Vienna Woods," and many other best-known waltzes and other dances. 160pp. 9 x 12.
0-486-27851-4

Sweelinck, Jan Pieterszoon, WORKS FOR ORGAN AND KEYBOARD. Nearly all of early Dutch composer's difficult-to-find keyboard works. Chorale variations; toccatas, fantasias; variations on secular, dance tunes. Also, incomplete and/or modified works, plus fantasia by John Bull. 272pp. 9 x 12.   0-486-24935-2

Telemann, Georg Philipp, THE 36 FANTASIAS FOR KEYBOARD. Graceful compositions by 18th-century master. 1923 Breslauer edition. 80pp. 8⅛ x 11.   0-486-25365-1

Tichenor, Trebor Jay, (ed.), RAGTIME RARITIES. 63 tuneful, rediscovered piano rags by 51 composers (or teams). Does not duplicate selections in *Classic Piano Rags* (Dover, 20469-3). 305pp. 9 x 12.
0-486-23157-7

Tichenor, Trebor Jay, (ed.), RAGTIME REDISCOVERIES. 64 unusual rags demonstrate diversity of style, local tradition. Original sheet music. 320pp. 9 x 12.   0-486-23776-1

Available from your music dealer or write for free Music Catalog to
Dover Publications, Inc., Dept. MUBI, 31 East 2nd Street, Mineola, NY 11501
Visit us online at www.doverpublications.com

Dover Opera, Choral and Lieder Scores

Bach, Johann Sebastian, EASTER ORATORIO IN FULL SCORE. Reproduces the authoritative Bach-Gesellschaft edition, in which the vocal parts of the third version of the oratorio were collated with the score of the first revision in an attempt to discover Bach's final intentions. Instrumentation. New English translation of text. 80pp. 9 x 12. 0-486-41890-1

Bach, Johann Sebastian, ELEVEN GREAT CANTATAS. Full vocal-instrumental score from Bach-Gesellschaft edition. *Christ lag in Todesbanden, Ich hatte viel Bekümmerniss, Jauchhzet Gott in allen Landen,* eight others. Study score. 350pp. 9 x 12. 0-486-23268-9

Bach, Johann Sebastian, MASS IN B MINOR IN FULL SCORE. The crowning glory of Bach's lifework in the field of sacred music and a universal statement of Christian faith, reprinted from the authoritative Bach-Gesellschaft edition. Translation of texts. 320pp. 9 x 12. 0-486-25992-7

Bach, Johann Sebastian, SEVEN GREAT SACRED CANTATAS IN FULL SCORE. Seven favorite sacred cantatas. Printed from a clear, modern engraving and sturdily bound; new literal line-for-line translations. Reliable Bach-Gesellschaft edition. Complete German texts. 256pp. 9 x 12. 0-486-24950-6

Bach, Johann Sebastian, SIX GREAT SECULAR CANTATAS IN FULL SCORE. Bach's nearest approach to comic opera. *Hunting Cantata, Wedding Cantata, Aeolus Appeased, Phoebus and Pan, Coffee Cantata,* and *Peasant Cantata.* 286pp. 9 x 12. 0-486-23934-9

Beethoven, Ludwig van, FIDELIO IN FULL SCORE. Beethoven's only opera, complete in one affordable volume, including all spoken German dialogue. Republication of C. F. Peters, Leipzig edition. 272pp. 9 x 12. 0-486-24740-6

Bizet, Georges, CARMEN IN FULL SCORE. Complete, authoritative score of perhaps the world's most popular opera, in the version most commonly performed today, with recitatives by Ernest Guiraud. 574pp. 9 x 12. 0-486-25820-3

Brahms, Johannes, COMPLETE SONGS FOR SOLO VOICE AND PIANO (two volumes). A total of 113 songs in complete score by greatest lieder writer since Schubert. Series I contains 15-song cycle *Die Schone Magelone*; Series II includes famous "Lullaby." Total of 448pp. 9⅜ x 12¼. Series I: 0-486-23820-2; Series II: 0-486-23821-0

Brahms, Johannes, COMPLETE SONGS FOR SOLO VOICE AND PIANO: Series III. 64 songs, published from 1877 to 1886, include such favorites as "Geheimnis," "Alte Liebe," and "Vergebliches Standchen." 224pp. 9 x 12. 0-486-23822-9

Brahms, Johannes, COMPLETE SONGS FOR SOLO VOICE AND PIANO: Series IV. 120 songs that complete the Brahms song oeuvre, with sensitive arrangements of 91 folk and traditional songs. 240pp. 9 x 12. 0-486-23823-7

Brahms, Johannes, GERMAN REQUIEM IN FULL SCORE. Definitive Breitkopf & Härtel edition of Brahms's greatest vocal work, fully scored for solo voices, mixed chorus and orchestra. 208pp. 9⅜ x 12¼. 0-486-25486-0

Debussy, Claude, PELLÉAS ET MÉLISANDE IN FULL SCORE. Reprinted from the E. Fromont (1904) edition, this volume faithfully reproduces the full orchestral-vocal score of Debussy's sole and enduring opera masterpiece. 416pp. 9 x 12. (Available in U.S. only) 0-486-24825-9

Debussy, Claude, SONGS, 1880–1904. Rich selection of 36 songs set to texts by Verlaine, Baudelaire, Pierre Louÿs, Charles d'Orleans, others. 175pp. 9 x 12. 0-486-24131-9

Fauré, Gabriel, SIXTY SONGS. "Clair de lune," "Apres un reve," "Chanson du pecheur," "Automne," and other great songs set for medium voice. Reprinted from French editions. 288pp. 8⅜ x 11. (Not available in France or Germany) 0-486-26534-X

Gilbert, W. S. and Sullivan, Sir Arthur, THE AUTHENTIC GILBERT & SULLIVAN SONGBOOK, 92 songs, uncut, original keys, in piano renderings approved by Sullivan. 399pp. 9 x 12. 0-486-23482-7

Gilbert, W. S. and Sullivan, Sir Arthur, HMS PINAFORE IN FULL SCORE. New edition by Carl Simpson and Ephraim Hammett Jones. Some of Gilbert's most clever flashes of wit and a number of Sullivan's most charming melodies in a handsome, authoritative new edition based on original manuscripts and early sources. 256pp. 9 x 12. 0-486-42201-1

Gilbert, W. S. and Sullivan, Sir Arthur (Carl Simpson and Ephraim Hammett Jones, eds.), THE PIRATES OF PENZANCE IN FULL SCORE. New performing edition corrects numerous errors, offers performers the choice of two versions of the Act II finale, and gives the first accurate full score of the "Climbing over Rocky Mountain" section. 288pp. 9 x 12. 0-486-41891-X

Grieg, Edvard, FIFTY SONGS FOR HIGH VOICE. Outstanding compilation includes many of his most popular melodies, such as "Solvejg's Song," "From Monte Pincio," and "Dreams." Introduction. Notes. 176pp. 9 x 12. 0-486-44130-X

Hale, Philip (ed.), FRENCH ART SONGS OF THE NINETEENTH CENTURY: 39 Works from Berlioz to Debussy. 39 songs from romantic period by 18 composers: Berlioz, Chausson, Debussy (six songs), Gounod, Massenet, Thomas, etc. French text, English singing translation for high voice. 182pp. 9 x 12. (Not available in France or Germany) 0-486-23680-3

Handel, George Frideric, GIULIO CESARE IN FULL SCORE. Great Baroque masterpiece reproduced directly from authoritative Deutsche Handelgesellschaft edition. Gorgeous melodies, inspired orchestration. Complete and unabridged. 160pp. 9⅜ x 12¼. 0-486-25056-3

Handel, George Frideric, MESSIAH IN FULL SCORE. An authoritative full-score edition of the oratorio that is the best-known, most-beloved, most-performed large-scale musical work in the English-speaking world. 240pp. 9 x 12. 0-486-26067-4

Monteverdi, Claudio, MADRIGALS: BOOK IV & V. 39 finest madrigals with new line-for-line literal English translations of the poems facing the Italian text. 256pp. 8⅛ x 11. (Available in U.S. only) 0-486-25102-0

Mozart, Wolfgang Amadeus, THE ABDUCTION FROM THE SERAGLIO IN FULL SCORE. Mozart's early comic masterpiece, exactingly reproduced from the authoritative Breitkopf & Härtel edition. 320pp. 9 x 12. 0-486-26004-6

Mozart, Wolfgang Amadeus, COSI FAN TUTTE IN FULL SCORE. Scholarly edition of one of Mozart's greatest operas. Da Ponte libretto. Commentary. Preface. Translated Front Matter. 448pp. 9⅜ x 12¼. (Available in U.S. only) 0-486-24528-4

Mozart, Wolfgang Amadeus, DON GIOVANNI: COMPLETE ORCHESTRAL SCORE. Full score that contains everything from the original version, along with later arias, recitatives, and duets added to original score for Vienna performance. Peters edition. Study score. 468pp. 9⅜ x 12¼. (Available in U.S. only) 0-486-23026-0

Mozart, Wolfgang Amadeus, THE MAGIC FLUTE (DIE ZAUBERFLÖTE) IN FULL SCORE. Authoritative C. F. Peters edition of Mozart's brilliant last opera still widely popular. Includes all the spoken dialogue. 226pp. 9 x 12. 0-486-24783-X

Mozart, Wolfgang Amadeus, THE MARRIAGE OF FIGARO: COMPLETE SCORE. Finest comic opera ever written. Full score, beautifully engraved, includes passages often cut in other editions. Peters edition. Study score. 448pp. 9⅜ x 12¼. (Available in U.S. only) 0-486-23751-6

*Available from your music dealer or write for **free** Music Catalog to*
Dover Publications, Inc., Dept. MUBI, 31 East 2nd Street, Mineola, NY 11501
*Visit us online at **www.doverpublications.com***

Dover Orchestral Scores

Bach, Johann Sebastian, COMPLETE CONCERTI FOR SOLO KEYBOARD AND ORCHESTRA IN FULL SCORE. Bach's seven complete concerti for solo keyboard and orchestra in full score from the authoritative Bach-Gesellschaft edition. 206pp. 9 x 12. 0-486-24929-8

Bach, Johann Sebastian, THE SIX BRANDENBURG CONCERTOS AND THE FOUR ORCHESTRAL SUITES IN FULL SCORE. Complete standard Bach-Gesellschaft editions in large, clear format. Study score. 273pp. 9 x 12. 0-486-23376-6

Bach, Johann Sebastian, THE THREE VIOLIN CONCERTI IN FULL SCORE. Concerto in A Minor, BWV 1041; Concerto in E Major, BWV 1042; and Concerto for Two Violins in D Minor, BWV 1043. Bach-Gesellschaft editions. 64pp. 9⅜ x 12¼. 0-486-25124-1

Beethoven, Ludwig van, COMPLETE PIANO CONCERTOS IN FULL SCORE. Complete scores of five great Beethoven piano concertos, with all cadenzas as he wrote them, reproduced from authoritative Breitkopf & Härtel edition. New Table of Contents. 384pp. 9⅜ x 12¼. 0-486-24563-2

Beethoven, Ludwig van, SIX GREAT OVERTURES IN FULL SCORE. Six staples of the orchestral repertoire from authoritative Breitkopf & Härtel edition. *Leonore Overtures,* Nos. 1–3; Overtures to *Coriolanus, Egmont, Fidelio.* 288pp. 9 x 12. 0-486-24789-9

Beethoven, Ludwig van, SYMPHONIES NOS. 1, 2, 3, AND 4 IN FULL SCORE. Republication of H. Litolff edition. 272pp. 9 x 12. 0-486-26033-X

Beethoven, Ludwig van, SYMPHONIES NOS. 5, 6 AND 7 IN FULL SCORE, Ludwig van Beethoven. Republication of H. Litolff edition. 272pp. 9 x 12. 0-486-26034-8

Beethoven, Ludwig van, SYMPHONIES NOS. 8 AND 9 IN FULL SCORE. Republication of H. Litolff edition. 256pp. 9 x 12. 0-486-26035-6

Beethoven, Ludwig van; Mendelssohn, Felix; and Tchaikovsky, Peter Ilyitch, GREAT ROMANTIC VIOLIN CONCERTI IN FULL SCORE. The Beethoven Op. 61, Mendelssohn Op. 64 and Tchaikovsky Op. 35 concertos reprinted from Breitkopf & Härtel editions. 224pp. 9 x 12. 0-486-24989-1

Borodin, Alexander, SYMPHONY NO. 2 IN B MINOR IN FULL SCORE. Rescored after its disastrous debut, the four movements offer a unified construction of dramatic contrasts in mood, color, and tempo. A beloved example of Russian nationalist music of the Romantic period. viii+152pp. 9 x 12. 0-486-44120-2

Brahms, Johannes, COMPLETE CONCERTI IN FULL SCORE. Piano Concertos Nos. 1 and 2; Violin Concerto, Op. 77; Concerto for Violin and Cello, Op. 102. Definitive Breitkopf & Härtel edition. 352pp. 9⅜ x 12¼. 0-486-24170-X

Brahms, Johannes, COMPLETE SYMPHONIES. Full orchestral scores in one volume. No. 1 in C Minor, Op. 68; No. 2 in D Major, Op. 73; No. 3 in F Major, Op. 90; and No. 4 in E Minor, Op. 98. Reproduced from definitive Vienna Gesellschaft der Musikfreunde edition. Study score. 344pp. 9 x 12. 0-486-23053-8

Brahms, Johannes, THREE ORCHESTRAL WORKS IN FULL SCORE: Academic Festival Overture, Tragic Overture and Variations on a Theme by Joseph Haydn. Reproduced from the authoritative Breitkopf & Härtel edition three of Brahms's great orchestral favorites. Editor's commentary in German and English. 112pp. 9⅜ x 12¼. 0-486-24637-X

Chopin, Frédéric, THE PIANO CONCERTOS IN FULL SCORE. The authoritative Breitkopf & Härtel full-score edition in one volume; Piano Concertos No. 1 in E Minor and No. 2 in F Minor. 176pp. 9 x 12. 0-486-25835-1

Corelli, Arcangelo, COMPLETE CONCERTI GROSSI IN FULL SCORE. All 12 concerti in the famous late nineteenth-century edition prepared by violinist Joseph Joachim and musicologist Friedrich Chrysander. 240pp. 8⅜ x 11¼. 0-486-25606-5

Debussy, Claude, THREE GREAT ORCHESTRAL WORKS IN FULL SCORE. Three of the Impressionist's most-recorded, most-performed favorites: *Prélude à l'Après-midi d'un Faune, Nocturnes,* and *La Mer.* Reprinted from early French editions. 279pp. 9 x 12. 0-486-24441-5

Dvořák, Antonín, SERENADE NO. 1, OP. 22, AND SERENADE NO. 2, OP. 44, IN FULL SCORE. Two works typified by elegance of form, intense harmony, rhythmic variety, and uninhibited emotionalism. 96pp. 9 x 12. 0-486-41895-2

Dvořák, Antonín, SYMPHONY NO. 8 IN G MAJOR, OP. 88, SYMPHONY NO. 9 IN E MINOR, OP. 95 ("NEW WORLD") IN FULL SCORE. Two celebrated symphonies by the great Czech composer, the Eighth and the immensely popular Ninth, "From the New World," in one volume. 272pp. 9 x 12. 0-486-24749-X

Elgar, Edward, CELLO CONCERTO IN E MINOR, OP. 85, IN FULL SCORE. A tour de force for any cellist, this frequently performed work is widely regarded as an elegy for a lost world. Melodic and evocative, it exhibits a remarkable scope, ranging from tragic passion to buoyant optimism. Reproduced from an authoritative source. 112pp. 8⅜ x 11. 0-486-41896-0

Franck, César, SYMPHONY IN D MINOR IN FULL SCORE. Superb, authoritative edition of Franck's only symphony, an often-performed and recorded masterwork of late French romantic style. 160pp. 9 x 12. 0-486-25373-2

Handel, George Frideric, COMPLETE CONCERTI GROSSI IN FULL SCORE. Monumental Opus 6 Concerti Grossi, Opus 3 and "Alexander's Feast" Concerti Grossi—19 in all—reproduced from the most authoritative edition. 258pp. 9⅜ x 12¼. 0-486-24187-4

Handel, George Frideric, WATER MUSIC AND MUSIC FOR THE ROYAL FIREWORKS IN FULL SCORE. Full scores of two of the most popular Baroque orchestral works performed today—reprinted from the definitive Deutsche Handelgesellschaft edition. Total of 96pp. 8⅛ x 11. 0-486-25070-9

Haydn, Joseph, SYMPHONIES 88–92 IN FULL SCORE: The Haydn Society Edition. Full score of symphonies Nos. 88 through 92. Large, readable noteheads, ample margins for fingerings, etc., and extensive Editor's Commentary. 304pp. 9 x 12. (Available in U.S. only) 0-486-24445-8

Mahler, Gustav, DAS LIED VON DER ERDE IN FULL SCORE. Mahler's masterpiece, a fusion of song and symphony, reprinted from the original 1912 Universal Edition. English translations of song texts. 160pp. 9 x 12. 0-486-25657-X

Mahler, Gustav, SYMPHONIES NOS. 1 AND 2 IN FULL SCORE. Unabridged, authoritative Austrian editions of Symphony No. 1 in D Major ("Titan") and Symphony No. 2 in C Minor ("Resurrection"). 384pp. 8⅛ x 11. 0-486-25473-9

Mahler, Gustav, SYMPHONIES NOS. 3 AND 4 IN FULL SCORE. Two brilliantly contrasting masterworks—one scored for a massive ensemble, the other for small orchestra and soloist—reprinted from authoritative Viennese editions. 368pp. 9⅜ x 12¼. 0-486-26166-2

Mahler, Gustav, SYMPHONY NO. 8 IN FULL SCORE. Authoritative edition of massive, complex "Symphony of a Thousand." Scored for orchestra, eight solo voices, double chorus, boys' choir and organ. Reprint of Izdatel'stvo "Muzyka," Moscow, edition. Translation of texts. 272pp. 9⅜ x 12¼. 0-486-26022-4

Mendelssohn, Felix, MAJOR ORCHESTRAL WORKS IN FULL SCORE. Considered to be Mendelssohn's finest orchestral works, here in one volume are the complete *Midsummer Night's Dream; Hebrides Overture; Calm Sea and Prosperous Voyage Overture;* Symphony No. 3 in A ("Scottish"); and Symphony No. 4 in A ("Italian"). Breitkopf & Härtel edition. Study score. 406pp. 9 x 12. 0-486-23184-4

Dover Orchestral Scores

Mozart, Wolfgang Amadeus, CONCERTI FOR WIND INSTRUMENTS IN FULL SCORE. Exceptional volume contains ten pieces for orchestra and wind instruments and includes some of Mozart's finest, most popular music. 272pp. 9⅜ x 12¼. 0-486-25228-0

Mozart, Wolfgang Amadeus, LATER SYMPHONIES. Full orchestral scores to last symphonies (Nos. 35–41) reproduced from definitive Breitkopf & Härtel Complete Works edition. Study score. 285pp. 9 x 12.
0-486-23052-X

Mozart, Wolfgang Amadeus, PIANO CONCERTOS NOS. 1–6 IN FULL SCORE. Reproduced complete and unabridged from the authoritative Breitkopf & Hartel Complete Works edition, it offers a revealing look at the development of a budding master. x+198pp. 9⅜ x 12¼. 0-486-44191-1

Mozart, Wolfgang Amadeus, PIANO CONCERTOS NOS. 11–16 IN FULL SCORE. Authoritative Breitkopf & Härtel edition of six staples of the concerto repertoire, including Mozart's cadenzas for Nos. 12–16. 256pp. 9⅜ x 12¼.
0-486-25468-2

Mozart, Wolfgang Amadeus, PIANO CONCERTOS NOS. 17–22 IN FULL SCORE. Six complete piano concertos in full score, with Mozart's own cadenzas for Nos. 17–19. Breitkopf & Härtel edition. Study score. 370pp. 9⅜ x 12¼. 0-486-23599-8

Mozart, Wolfgang Amadeus, PIANO CONCERTOS NOS. 23–27 IN FULL SCORE. Mozart's last five piano concertos in full score, plus cadenzas for Nos. 23 and 27, and the Concert Rondo in D Major, K.382. Breitkopf & Härtel edition. Study score. 310pp. 9⅜ x 12¼. 0-486-23600-5

Mozart, Wolfgang Amadeus, 17 DIVERTIMENTI FOR VARIOUS INSTRUMENTS. Sparkling pieces of great vitality and brilliance from 1771 to 1779; consecutively numbered from 1 to 17. Reproduced from definitive Breitkopf & Härtel Complete Works edition. Study score. 241pp. 9⅜ x 12¼.
0-486-23862-8

Mozart, Wolfgang Amadeus, THE VIOLIN CONCERTI AND THE SINFONIA CONCERTANTE, K.364, IN FULL SCORE. All five violin concerti and famed double concerto reproduced from authoritative Breitkopf & Härtel Complete Works Edition. 208pp. 9⅜ x 12¼. 0-486-25169-1

Paganini, Nicolo and Wieniawski, Henri, PAGANINI'S VIOLIN CONCERTO NO. 1 IN D MAJOR, OP. 6, AND WIENIAWSKI'S VIOLIN CONCERTO NO. 2 IN D MINOR, OP. 22, IN FULL SCORE. This outstanding new edition brings together two of the most popular and most performed violin concertos of the Romantic repertoire in one convenient, moderately priced volume. 208pp. 8⅜ x 11. 0-486-43151-7

Ravel, Maurice, DAPHNIS AND CHLOE IN FULL SCORE. Definitive full-score edition of Ravel's rich musical setting of a Greek fable by Longus is reprinted here from the original French edition. 320pp. 9⅜ x 12¼. (Not available in France or Germany) 0-486-25826-2

Ravel, Maurice, LE TOMBEAU DE COUPERIN and VALSES NOBLES ET SENTIMENTALES IN FULL SCORE. *Le Tombeau de Couperin* consists of "Prelude," "Forlane," "Menuet," and "Rigaudon"; the uninterrupted 8 waltzes of *Valses Nobles et Sentimentales* abound with lilting rhythms and unexpected harmonic subtleties. 144pp. 9⅜ x 12¼. (Not available in France or Germany) 0-486-41898-7

Ravel, Maurice, RAPSODIE ESPAGNOLE, MOTHER GOOSE and PAVANE FOR A DEAD PRINCESS IN FULL SCORE. Full authoritative scores of 3 enormously popular works by the great French composer, each rich in orchestral settings. 160pp. 9⅜ x 12¼. 0-486-41899-5

Saint-Saens, Camille, DANSE MACABRE AND HAVANAISE FOR VIOLIN AND ORCHESTRA IN FULL SCORE. Two of Saint-Saens' most popular works appear in this affordable volume: the symphonic poem about the dance of death, *Danse Macabre,* and *Havanaise,* a piece inspired by a Cuban dance that highlights its languid mood with bursts of virtuosity. iv+92pp. 9 x 12. 0-486-44147-4

Schubert, Franz, FOUR SYMPHONIES IN FULL SCORE. Schubert's four most popular symphonies: No. 4 in C Minor ("Tragic"); No. 5 in B-flat Major; No. 8 in B Minor ("Unfinished"); and No. 9 in C Major ("Great"). Breitkopf & Härtel edition. Study score. 261pp. 9⅜ x 12¼. 0-486-23681-1

Schubert, Franz, SYMPHONY NO. 3 IN D MAJOR AND SYMPHONY NO. 6 IN C MAJOR IN FULL SCORE. The former is scored for 12 wind instruments and timpani; the latter is known as "The Little Symphony in C" to distinguish it from Symphony No. 9, "The Great Symphony in C." Authoritative editions. 128pp. 9⅜ x 12¼. 0-486-42134-1

Schumann, Robert, COMPLETE SYMPHONIES IN FULL SCORE. No. 1 in B-flat Major, Op. 38 ("Spring"); No. 2 in C Major, Op. 61; No. 3 in E-flat Major, Op. 97 ("Rhenish"); and No. 4 in D Minor, Op. 120. Breitkopf & Härtel editions. Study score. 416pp. 9⅜ x 12¼. 0-486-24013-4

Strauss, Johann, Jr., THE GREAT WALTZES IN FULL SCORE. Complete scores of eight melodic masterpieces: "The Beautiful Blue Danube," "Emperor Waltz," "Tales of the Vienna Woods," "Wiener Blut," and four more. Authoritative editions. 336pp. 8⅜ x 11¼. 0-486-26009-7

Strauss, Richard, TONE POEMS, SERIES I: DON JUAN, TOD UND VERKLARUNG, and DON QUIXOTE IN FULL SCORE. Three of the most often performed and recorded works in entire orchestral repertoire, reproduced in full score from original editions. 286pp. 9⅜ x 12¼. (Available in U.S. only) 0-486-23754-0

Strauss, Richard, TONE POEMS, SERIES II: TILL EULENSPIEGELS LUSTIGE STREICHE, "ALSO SPRACH ZARATHUSTRA," and EIN HELDENLEBEN IN FULL SCORE. Three important orchestral works, including very popular *Till Eulenspiegel's Merry Pranks,* reproduced in full score from original editions. Study score. 315pp. 9⅜ x 12¼. (Available in U.S. only) 0-486-23755-9

Stravinsky, Igor, THE FIREBIRD IN FULL SCORE (Original 1910 Version). Inexpensive edition of modern masterpiece, renowned for brilliant orchestration, glowing color. Authoritative Russian edition. 176pp. 9⅜ x 12¼. (Available in U.S. only) 0-486-25535-2

Stravinsky, Igor, PETRUSHKA IN FULL SCORE: Original Version. Full-score edition of Stravinsky's masterful score for the great Ballets Russes 1911 production of *Petrushka.* 160pp. 9⅜ x 12¼. (Available in U.S. only) 0-486-25680-4

Stravinsky, Igor, THE RITE OF SPRING IN FULL SCORE. Full-score edition of most famous musical work of the 20th century, created as a ballet score for Diaghilev's Ballets Russes. 176pp. 9⅜ x 12¼. (Available in U.S. only) 0-486-25857-2

Tchaikovsky, Peter Ilyitch, FOURTH, FIFTH AND SIXTH SYMPHONIES IN FULL SCORE. Complete orchestral scores of Symphony No. 4 in F Minor, Op. 36; Symphony No. 5 in E Minor, Op. 64; Symphony No. 6 in B Minor, "Pathetique," Op. 74. Study score. Breitkopf & Härtel editions. 480pp. 9⅜ x 12¼. 0-486-23861-X

Tchaikovsky, Peter Ilyitch, NUTCRACKER SUITE IN FULL SCORE. Among the most popular ballet pieces ever created; available in a complete, inexpensive, high-quality score to study and enjoy. 128pp. 9 x 12.
0-486-25379-1

von Weber, Carl Maria, GREAT OVERTURES IN FULL SCORE. Overtures to *Oberon, Der Freischutz, Euryanthe* and *Preciosa* reprinted from authoritative Breitkopf & Härtel editions. 112pp. 9 x 12. 0-486-25225-6

*Available from your music dealer or write for **free** Music Catalog to*
Dover Publications, Inc., Dept. MUBI, 31 East 2nd Street, Mineola, NY 11501
*Visit us online at **www.doverpublications.com***

Dover Popular Songbooks

(Arranged by title)

ALEXANDER'S RAGTIME BAND AND OTHER FAVORITE SONG HITS, 1901–1911, David A. Jasen (ed.). Fifty vintage popular songs America still sings, reprinted in their entirety from the original editions. Introduction. 224pp. 9 x 12. (Available in U.S. only) 0-486-25331-7

AMERICAN BALLADS AND FOLK SONGS, John A. Lomax and Alan Lomax. Over 200 songs, music and lyrics: "Frankie and Albert," "John Henry," "Frog Went a-Courtin'," "Down in the Valley," "Skip to My Lou," other favorites. Notes on each song. 672pp. 5⅜ x 8½. 0-486-28276-7

AMERICAN FOLK SONGS FOR GUITAR, David Nadal (ed.). Forty-nine classics for beginning and intermediate guitar players, including "Beautiful Dreamer," "Amazing Grace," "Aura Lee," "John Henry," "The Gift to Be Simple," "Go Down, Moses," "Sweet Betsy from Pike," "Short'nin Bread," many more. 96pp. 9 x 12. 0-486-41700-X

THE AMERICAN SONG TREASURY: 100 Favorites, Theodore Raph (ed.). Complete piano arrangements, guitar chords, and lyrics for 100 best-loved tunes, "Buffalo Gals," "Oh, Suzanna," "Clementine," "Camptown Races," and much more. 416pp. 8⅜ x 11. 0-486-25222-1

"BEALE STREET" AND OTHER CLASSIC BLUES: 38 Works, 1901–1921, David A. Jasen (ed.). "St. Louis Blues," "The Hesitating Blues," "Down Home Blues," "Jelly Roll Blues," "Railroad Blues," and many more. Reproduced directly from rare sheet music (including original covers). Introduction. 160pp. 9 x 12. (Available in U.S. only) 0-486-40183-9

THE CIVIL WAR SONGBOOK, Richard Crawford (ed.). 37 songs: "Battle Hymn of the Republic," "Drummer Boy of Shiloh," "Dixie," and 34 more. 157pp. 9 x 12. 0-486-23422-3

CIVIL WAR SONGS AND BALLADS FOR GUITAR, Compiled, Edited, and Arranged by Jerry Silverman. 41 favorites, among them "Marching Through Georgia," "The Battle Hymn of the Republic," "Tenting on the Old Camp Ground," and "When Johnny Comes Marching Home." 160pp. 9 x 12. 0-486-41902-9

FAVORITE CHRISTMAS CAROLS, selected and arranged by Charles J. F. Cofone. Title, music, first verse and refrain of 34 traditional carols in handsome calligraphy; also subsequent verses and other information in type. 79pp. 8⅜ x 11. 0-486-20445-6

FAVORITE SONGS OF THE NINETIES, Robert Fremont (ed.). 88 favorites: "Ta-Ra-Ra-Boom-De-Aye," "The Band Played on," "Bird in a Gilded Cage," etc. 401pp. 9 x 12. 0-486-21536-9

500 BEST-LOVED SONG LYRICS, Ronald Herder (ed.). Complete lyrics for well-known folk songs, hymns, popular and show tunes, more. "Oh Susanna," "The Battle Hymn of the Republic," "When Johnny Comes Marching Home," hundreds more. Indispensable for singalongs, parties, family get-togethers, etc. 416pp. 5⅜ x 8½. 0-486-29725-X

MY FIRST BOOK OF AMERICAN FOLK SONGS: 20 Favorite Pieces in Easy Piano Arrangements, Bergerac (ed.). Expert settings of traditional favorites by a well-known composer and arranger for young pianists: *Amazing Grace, Blue Tail Fly, Sweet Betsy from Pike*, many more. 48pp. 8¼ x 11. 0-486-28885-4

MY FIRST BOOK OF CHRISTMAS SONGS: 20 Favorite Songs in Easy Piano Arrangements, Bergerac (ed.). Beginners will love playing these beloved favorites in easy arrangements: "Jingle Bells," "Deck the Halls," "Joy to the World," "Silent Night," "Away in a Manger," "Hark! The Herald Angels Sing," 14 more. Illustrations. 48pp. 8¼ x 11. 0-486-29718-7

NURSERY RHYMES AND NURSERY SONGS, J. W. Elliott. Classic collection of nursery rhymes set to music was, for decades, one of the most beloved of children's songbooks. J. W. Elliott's melodies perfectly capture the charms of these verses; many, including "Sing a Song of Sixpence," have become inseparable from the original rhymes. Lavishly illustrated with 66 beautiful engravings by the Dalziel brothers—renowned Victorian-era illustrators of children's books. 128pp. 8⅜ x 11. 0-486-43806-6

ONE HUNDRED ENGLISH FOLKSONGS, Cecil J. Sharp (ed.). Border ballads, folksongs, collected from all over Great Britain. "Lord Bateman," "Henry Martin," "The Green Wedding," many others. Piano. 235pp. 9 x 12. 0-486-23192-5

"PEG O' MY HEART" AND OTHER FAVORITE SONG HITS, 1912 & 1913, Stanley Appelbaum (ed.). 36 songs by Berlin, Herbert, Handy and others, with complete lyrics, full piano arrangements and original sheet music covers in black and white. 176pp. 9 x 12. 0-486-25998-6

PETRIE'S COMPLETE IRISH MUSIC: 1,582 Traditional Melodies, George Petrie (ed.). The work of 100 years and three generations of archivists, this compilation, which originally appeared in 1905, encompasses the musical wealth of a nation. 448pp. 8⅜ x 11. 0-486-43080-4

POPULAR IRISH SONGS, Florence Leniston (ed.). 37 all-time favorites with vocal and piano arrangements: "My Wild Irish Rose," "Irish Eyes are Smiling," "Last Rose of Summer," "Danny Boy," many more. 160pp. 0-486-26755-5

"A PRETTY GIRL IS LIKE A MELODY" AND OTHER FAVORITE SONG HITS, 1918–1919, David A. Jasen (ed.). "After You've Gone," "How Ya Gonna Keep 'Em Down on the Farm," "I'm Always Chasing Rainbows," "Rock-a-Bye Your Baby" and 36 other Golden Oldies. 176pp. 9 x 12. 0-486-29421-8

A RUSSIAN SONG BOOK, Rose N. Rubin and Michael Stillman (eds.). 25 traditional folk songs, plus 19 popular songs by twentieth-century composers. Full piano arrangements, guitar chords. Lyrics in original Cyrillic, transliteration and English translation. With discography. 112pp. 9 x 12. 0-486-26118-2

"THE ST. LOUIS BLUES" AND OTHER SONG HITS OF 1914, Sandy Marrone (ed.). Full vocal and piano for "By the Beautiful Sea," "Play a Simple Melody," "They Didn't Believe Me,"–21 songs in all. 112pp. 9 x 12. 0-486-26383-5

SEVENTY SCOTTISH SONGS, Helen Hopekirk (ed.). Complete piano and vocals for classics of Scottish song: *Flow Gently, Sweet Afton, Comin' thro' the Rye (Gin a Body Meet a Body), The Campbells are Comin', Robin Adair*, many more. 208pp. 8⅜ x 11. 0-486-27029-7

SONGS OF THE CIVIL WAR, Irwin Silber (ed.). Piano, vocal, guitar chords for 125 songs including "Battle Cry of Freedom," "Marching Through Georgia," "Dixie," "Oh, I'm a Good Old Rebel," "The Drummer Boy of Shiloh," many more. 400pp. 8⅜ x 11. 0-486-28438-7

STEPHEN FOSTER SONG BOOK, Stephen Foster. 40 favorites: "Beautiful Dreamer," "Camptown Races," "Jeanie with the Light Brown Hair," "My Old Kentucky Home," etc. 224pp. 9 x 12. 0-486-23048-1

35 SONG HITS BY GREAT BLACK SONGWRITERS: Bert Williams, Eubie Blake, Ernest Hogan and Others, David A. Jasen (ed.). Ballads, show tunes, other early 20th-century works by black songwriters include "Some of These Days," "A Good Man Is Hard to Find," "I'm Just Wild About Harry," "Love Will Find a Way," 31 other classics. Reprinted from rare sheet music, original covers. 160pp. 9 x 12. (Available in U.S. only) 0-486-40416-1

Available from your music dealer or write for free Music Catalog to
Dover Publications, Inc., Dept. MUBI, 31 East 2nd Street, Mineola, NY 11501
Visit us online at www.doverpublications.com

Dover Chamber Music Scores

Bach, Johann Sebastian, COMPLETE SUITES FOR UNACCOMPANIED CELLO AND SONATAS FOR VIOLA DA GAMBA. Bach-Gesellschaft edition of the six cello suites (BWV 1007–1012) and three sonatas (BWV 1027–1029), commonly played today on the cello. 112pp. 9⅜ x 12¼. 0-486-25641-3

Bach, Johann Sebastian, WORKS FOR VIOLIN. Complete Sonatas and Partitas for Unaccompanied Violin; Six Sonatas for Violin and Clavier. Bach-Gesellschaft edition. 158pp. 9⅜ x 12¼. 0-486-23683-8

Bartók, Béla, STRING QUARTETS NOS. 1 AND 2. The stirring first quartet captures the composer's great stylistic rebirth, from the Romanticism of the opening movement to a finale inspired by Hungarian folk tunes. The second quartet combines disparate influences into a work of astonishing force and originality. 96pp. 83/8 x 11. (Not available in Europe or United Kingdom.) 0-486-43799-X

Beethoven, Ludwig van. COMPLETE SONATAS AND VARIATIONS FOR CELLO AND PIANO. All five sonatas and three sets of variations. Breitkopf & Härtel edition. 176pp. 9⅜ x 12¼. 0-486-26441-6

Beethoven, Ludwig van. COMPLETE STRING QUARTETS, Breitkopf & Härtel edition. Six quartets of Opus 18; three quartets of Opus 59; Opera 74, 95, 127, 130, 131, 132, 135 and Grosse Fuge. Study score. 434pp. 9⅜ x 12¼. 0-486-22361-2

Beethoven, Ludwig van. COMPLETE VIOLIN SONATAS. All ten sonatas including the "Kreutzer" and "Spring" sonatas in the definitive Breitkopf & Härtel edition. 256pp. 9 x 12. 0-486-26277-4

Beethoven, Ludwig van. SIX GREAT PIANO TRIOS IN FULL SCORE. Definitive Breitkopf & Härtel edition of Beethoven's Piano Trios Nos. 1–6 including the "Ghost" and the "Archduke." 224pp. 9⅜ x 12¼. 0-486-25398-8

Brahms, Johannes, COMPLETE CHAMBER MUSIC FOR STRINGS AND CLARINET QUINTET. Vienna Gesellschaft der Musikfreunde edition of all quartets, quintets, and sextets without piano. Study edition. 262pp. 8⅝ x 11¼. 0-486-21914-3

Brahms, Johannes, COMPLETE PIANO TRIOS. All five piano trios in the definitive Breitkopf & Härtel edition. 288pp. 9 x 12. 0-486-25769-X

Brahms, Johannes, COMPLETE SONATAS FOR SOLO INSTRUMENT AND PIANO. All seven sonatas—three for violin, two for cello and two for clarinet (or viola)—reprinted from the authoritative Breitkopf & Härtel edition. 208pp. 9 x 12. 0-486-26091-7

Brahms, Johannes, QUINTET AND QUARTETS FOR PIANO AND STRINGS. Full scores of *Quintet in F Minor,* Op. 34; *Quartet in G Minor,* Op. 25; *Quartet in A Major,* Op. 26; *Quartet in C Minor,* Op. 60. Breitkopf & Härtel edition. 298pp. 9 x 12. 0-486-24900-X

Debussy, Claude and Ravel, Maurice, STRING QUARTETS BY DEBUSSY AND RAVEL/Claude Debussy: Quartet in G Minor, Op. 10/Maurice Ravel: Quartet in F Major. Authoritative one-volume edition of two influential masterpieces noted for individuality, delicate and subtle beauties. 112pp. 8⅛ x 11. (Not available in France or Germany) 0-486-25231-0

Dvořák, Antonín, FIVE LATE STRING QUARTETS. Treasury of Czech master's finest chamber works: Nos. 10, 11, 12, 13, 14. Reliable Simrock editions. 282pp. 8⅛ x 11. 0-486-25135-7

Haydn, Joseph, ELEVEN LATE STRING QUARTETS. Complete reproductions of Op. 74, Nos. 1–3; Op. 76, Nos. 1–6; and Op. 77, Nos. 1 and 2. Definitive Eulenburg edition. Full-size study score. 320pp. 8⅜ x 11¼. 0-486-23753-2

Haydn, Joseph, STRING QUARTETS, OPP. 20 and 33, COMPLETE. Complete reproductions of the 12 masterful quartets (six each) of Opp. 20 and 33—in the reliable Eulenburg edition. 272pp. 8⅜ x 11¼. 0-486-24852-6

Haydn, Joseph, STRING QUARTETS, OPP. 42, 50 and 54. Complete reproductions of Op. 42 in D Minor; Op. 50, Nos. 1–6 ("Prussian Quartets") and Op. 54, Nos. 1–3. Reliable Eulenburg edition. 224pp. 8⅜ x 11¼. 0-486-24262-5

Haydn, Joseph, TWELVE STRING QUARTETS. 12 often-performed works: Op. 55, Nos. 1–3 (including *Razor*); Op. 64, Nos. 1–6; Op. 71, Nos. 1–3. Definitive Eulenburg edition. 288pp. 8⅜ x 11¼. 0-486-23933-0

Mendelssohn, Felix, COMPLETE CHAMBER MUSIC FOR STRINGS. All of Mendelssohn's chamber music: Octet, Two Quintets, Six Quartets, and Four Pieces for String Quartet. (Nothing with piano is included.) Complete works edition (1874–7). Study score. 283pp. 9⅜ x 12¼. 0-486-23679-X

Mozart, Wolfgang Amadeus, COMPLETE STRING QUARTETS. Breitkopf & Härtel edition. All 23 string quartets plus alternate slow movement to K.156. Study score. 277pp. 9⅜ x 12¼. 0-486-22372-8

Mozart, Wolfgang Amadeus, COMPLETE STRING QUINTETS, Wolfgang Amadeus Mozart. All the standard-instrumentation string quintets, plus String Quintet in C Minor, K.406; Quintet with Horn or Second Cello, K.407; and Clarinet Quintet, K.581. Breitkopf & Härtel edition. Study score. 181pp. 9⅜ x 12¼. 0-486-23603-X

Ravel, Maurice, PIANO TRIO, MALLARMÉ POEMS AND OTHER CHAMBER WORKS. The celebrated *Piano Trio* of 1914, the *Mallarmé Poems* (1913), *Sonata for Violin and Cello* (1922), and *Introduction and Allegro* (1905) for harp and ensemble appear in this first-time collection of some of the composer's finest and most musically ambitious achievements in a single large-format volume. 128pp. 8⅜ x 11. (Not available in France or Germany) 0-486-43807-4

Schoenberg, Arnold, CHAMBER SYMPHONY NO. 1 FOR 15 SOLO INSTRUMENTS, OP. 9. One of Schoenberg's most pleasing and accessible works, this 1906 piece concentrates all the elements of a symphony into a single movement. 160 pp. 8⅜ x 11. (Available in U.S. only) 0-486-41900-2

Schubert, Franz, COMPLETE CHAMBER MUSIC FOR PIANOFORTE AND STRINGS. Breitkopf & Härtel edition. *Trout,* Quartet in F Major, and trios for piano, violin, cello. Study score. 192pp. 9 x 12. 0-486-21527-X

Schubert, Franz, COMPLETE CHAMBER MUSIC FOR STRINGS. Reproduced from famous Breitkopf & Härtel edition: Quintet in C Major (1828), 15 quartets and two trios for violin(s), viola, and violincello. Study score. 348pp. 9 x 12. 0-486-21463-X

Schumann, Clara (ed.), CHAMBER MUSIC OF ROBERT SCHUMANN, Superb collection of three trios, four quartets, and piano quintet. Breitkopf & Härtel edition. 288pp. 9⅜ x 12¼. 0-486-24101-7

Stravinsky, Igor, PRIBAOUTKI, RENARD AND RAGTIME FOR ELEVEN INSTRUMENTS. *Pribaoutki* (Nonsense Rhymes) is a set of four witty, brief songs for solo voice and eight solo instruments; *Renard,* adapted from Russian folktales, features talking animals; and *Ragtime for Eleven Instruments* reflects the composer's interest in the contemporary jazz idiom. Texts in Russian, French, German. 224pp. 8⅜ x 11. (Available in U.S. only) 0-486-41395-0

Tchaikovsky, Peter Ilyitch, PIANO TRIO IN A MINOR, OP. 50. Charming homage to pianist Nicholas Rubinstein. Distinctively Russian in character, with overtones of regional folk music and dance. Authoritative edition. 120pp. 8⅛ x 11. 0-486-42136-8

Tchaikovsky, Peter Ilyitch and Borodin, Alexander, COMPLETE STRING QUARTETS. Tchaikovsky's Quartets Nos. 1–3 and Borodin's Quartets Nos. 1 and 2, reproduced from authoritative editions. 240pp. 8⅜ x 11¼. 0-486-28333-X

*Available from your music dealer or write for **free** Music Catalog to*
Dover Publications, Inc., Dept. MUBI, 31 East 2nd Street, Mineola, NY 11501
*Visit us online at **www.doverpublications.com***